# AFTER PILKINGT(

This volume contains the original screenpl
of *Butley* and *Quartermaine's Terms*. It is
author and stills from the film.

hor

## SIMON GRAY

SIMON GRAY was born on Hayling Island in 1936 and educated at Portsmouth Grammar School and Westminster, then at universities in Canada and France before reading English at Cambridge. For twenty years he was a lecturer in English Literature at Queen Mary College, London. He has written a number of novels and television plays including *Sleeping Dog, Death of a Teddy Bear,* for which he won the Writers' Guild Award, *Pig in a Poke, Man in a Side-Car, Two Sundays* and *Plaintiffs and Defendants.* Since his first stage-play, *Wise Child* (1967), he has written *Dutch Uncle* (1969), an adaptation of *The Idiot* for the National Theatre (1970), *Spoiled* (1971) and *Butley*, which won the *Evening Standard* Best Play award for 1971. *Otherwise Engaged* won both the *Evening Standard* and *Plays and Players* Best Play awards for 1975. Subsequent stage plays have been *Dog Days* (Oxford Playhouse, 1976), *Molly* (Watford Palace, 1977; Comedy Theatre, 1978), *The Rear Column* (Globe Theatre, 1978), *Close of Play* (National Theatre, 1979), *Stage Struck* (Vaudeville Theatre, 1979), *Quartermaine's Terms* (Queen's Theatre, 1981, the only play ever to win the Cheltenham Prize for Literature), a version of Molière *Tartuffe* (Kennedy Center, Washington, 1982) and *The Common Pursuit* (Lyric Theatre, Hammersmith, 1984 and Long Wharf Theatre, Newhaven, U.S.A.) A revised version of *The Common Pursuit* was performed at the Matrix Theatre, Los Angeles in 1986, and in October 1986 Simon Gray co-directed a production for the Promenade Theatre, New York.

*The cover photographs from the BBC-TV production of* AFTER PILKINGTON *were taken by Nobby Clark. The front cover shows Bob Peck as* James Westgate. *The back cover shows Bob Peck and Miranda Richardson as* Penny.

*by the same author*

*Plays*

SLEEPING DOG
WISE CHILD
DUTCH UNCLE
SPOILED
THE IDIOT
BUTLEY
OTHERWISE ENGAGED, TWO SUNDAYS *and* PLAINTIFFS AND DEFENDANTS
DOG DAYS
THE REAR COLUMN, MOLLY *and* MAN IN A SIDE-CAR
CLOSE OF PLAY *and* PIG IN A POKE
STAGE STRUCK
QUARTERMAINE'S TERMS
THE COMMON PURSUIT
PLAYS: ONE (Butley, Otherwise Engaged, The Rear Column, Quartermaine's Terms, The Common Pursuit)

*Novels*

COLMAIN
LITTLE PORTIA
SIMPLE PEOPLE
A COMEBACK FOR STARK (under the pseudonym Hamish Reade)

*Prose*

AN UNNATURAL PURSUIT
*An account of the production of The Common Pursuit*

*Translation*

Tartuffe *by Molière*

# AFTER PILKINGTON

## SIMON GRAY

A Methuen Paperback

## A METHUEN THEATRESCRIPT

First published in Great Britain in 1987 as a Methuen paperback original by Methuen London Ltd, 11 New Fetter Lane, London EC4P 4EE, and in the United States of America by Methuen Inc, 29 West 35th Street, New York, NY 10001.

Photographs reproduced by courtesy of Nobby Clark and the BBC.

Set in IBM 10 pt Press Roman by 🅏 Tek-Art Ltd, Croydon, Surrey

Printed in Great Britain by
Richard Clay Ltd, Bungay, Suffolk

British Library Cataloguing in Publication Data
Gray, Simon
    After Pilkington. – (A Methuen theatrescript)
    I. Title
    822'.914        PR6057.R33
    ISBN 0-413-15290-1

# INTRODUCTION

Many years ago I was invited to adapt a kind of Jamesian ghost-thriller into a film script. I spent months wrestling with the project — my problem being that, though I'd found the plot perfectly credible while reading it as a novel, I didn't believe a word of it while writing it as a film. I began to change it, quite radically, although nowhere near radically enough. The consequence was that after several drafts I was stuck with a story that was in part wholly mine — the characters, dialogue, setting, etc. — and a structure that still belonged to somebody else. The film, needless to say, never got made, and I buried, but never quite forgot, the script. A year or so ago, during a phase when as usual I had nothing particular to do, I picked it out of its box, shuffled through the old pages, discarded everything that derived from the original, threw away most of what was my own, and started again, from nothing, so to speak, except a growing idea of the two central characters, and a desire to be unpleasantly shocking — to be frightening, if I could manage it. The new story, now completely detached from the book and only containing echoes here and there of my past scripts, emerged in little lumps, but didn't cohere until one morning, in Eastbourne, where I'd gone to finish it, I found myself thinking of a certain actor with whom I've worked once or twice, and a particular expression he employs occasionally, and to terrific effect, in his work: an expression of enigmatic diffidence, which transforms his face from blandly occidental to something almost oriental. Cunning diffidence struck me as being the key to the real nature of my central character, and everything — his lies, his crimes, his final ruthless tenderness — flowed from that. The woman in question rose perfectly naturally as the proper opposition that would release a story that was simultaneously his and hers. Theirs. A horror story that was full of victims of all sorts. At the last it was great fun to write. I hope it is fun on the screen, and fun to read. And that it frightens the hell out of people, naturally.

Simon Gray
*Summer 1986*

*Above:* Porker (James) in pursuit of Patch (Penny).

*Below:* Derek succumbing to James's plot, in Hall, with James's uncle 'Pottsy', Master of the College.

*Above:* James making further excuses to Amanda.

*Below:* Porker (James) spotting his quarry, Patch (Penny).

*Right:* Patch (Penny) pensive before her confession.

*Above:* Porker (James) searching for a glimpse of Patch (Penny).

*Below:* James taking deceitful farewell of Amanda.

*Right:* Derek, as we never see him, in his off-screen togs.

*Above:* Derek, as he might be, conducting an informal seminar.

*Below:* James peering into lecture room.

# AFTER PILKINGTON

*After Pilkington* was produced by Kenith Trodd and broadcast in 1987. The cast was as follows:

| | |
|---|---|
| JAMES | Bob Peck |
| PENNY | Miranda Richardson |
| DEREK | Barry Foster |
| BORIS | Gary Waldhorn |
| DEIRDRE | Mary Miller |
| AMANDA | Reina James |
| WILKINS | Richard Brenner |
| POTTS | John Gill |
| DOCTOR | Nigel Nevinson |
| YOUNG PENNY | Sarah Butler |
| YOUNG JAMES | Richard Grant |
| PILKINGTON | Derek Ware |

*Technical Credits*

| | |
|---|---|
| Director | CHRISTOPHER MORAHAN |
| Producer | KEN TRODD |
| Production Associate | ANNA KALNARS |
| Production Managers | LIZ TRUBRIDGE |
| | MIKE FEWINGS |
| Production Assistants | EILEEN KEIGHTLEY |
| | PAMELA HOSSICK |
| Assistant Floor Manager | ANGELA BEAUMONT |
| Designer | GRAEME THOMSON |
| Properties Buyer | ROBIN RUMBELOW |
| Artists' Booker | ANNE HOPKINSON |
| Costume Designer | CATRIONA TOMALIN |
| Make-up | CHRISTINE POWERS |
| Film Cameraman | ANDREW DUNN |
| Assistant Cameraman | GILES NUTTGENS |
| Sound Recordist | GRAHAM ROFF |
| Assistant Sound Recordist | TREVOR GOSLING |
| Film Editor | DAN RAE |

## 1. Exterior. The High. Oxford. Day.

*From Carfax Tower a panning shot of Oxford spires to see cyclists in The High. They pass The Mitre.*

*In the Turl. JAMES stops at a bookshop. He picks out a book, a collection of poems by Herrick. He opens it, looks through it rapidly and puts the book back.*

*As he looks up, see PENNY from his point of view and glimpsed through the traffic. She is on a bicycle on the far side of The High. Her face is only momentarily visible under a straw hat. See her go out with the traffic and out of sight.*

*Cut from JAMES to little glimpses of music over of Schubert's 'The Trout' begins. It is as if this is a continuation of the previous scene:*

## 2. Interior. Oxford concert hall. Day.

*'The Trout' continues. See PENNY in the front row from JAMES's point of view, far back in the hall.*

*Cut from JAMES to little glimpses of PENNY as she occasionally turns her head, listening to the music which is nearing its end.*

*Take in JAMES's hand, a woman's hand on it. He turns his head and see (from his point of view), AMANDA. She smiles at him. He smiles back, then looks again towards PENNY.*

*We have a glimpse of her as the music reaches its climax, and on that glimpse:*

## 3. Interior. Oxford psychological laboratory.

*JAMES pushes the door of a laboratory open. There is an aisle of cages made of glass and wire which evidently contain a variety of animals judging from the sounds they emit; they are not seen during the scene.*

*BORIS, in shirt-sleeves, is bent at a cage at the end of the aisle, jotting something into a notebook. He is about five years older than JAMES with the slightest hint of a middle-European accent.*

BORIS: You're late.

JAMES: Untrue. It's exactly five.

BORIS (*looks at his watch*): Yes. I must have decided you were going to funk it.

*BORIS goes into his office at the end of the aisle, on which 'Dr Boris Heinz' is inscribed. He takes off his white coat and puts on a jacket.*

*JAMES, meanwhile, is peering into a cage. He shudders, passes on and looks into another cage.*

JAMES: Why should I funk it?

BORIS: Because you're going to hate this guy.

*JAMES, with an expression of slight disgust, passes on to the next cage.*

JAMES: I thought you said he was your oldest friend.

*BORIS, emerging from his office, is adjusting various temperature controls etc. by the office.*

BORIS: Oldest *living* friend.

JAMES: And you said he was a bit of a charmer.

BORIS: No, charmless. I said completely charmless.

JAMES (*not really listening*): What's this?

BORIS: A rabbit.

JAMES: Yes, I can see it's a rabbit. But what's it eating?

BORIS (*looks*): Pigs' kidneys, they look like. Yes, pigs' kidneys. One of my research students is trying to induce a primitive form of schizophrenia. Probably all she'll get in the end is a carnivorous rabbit. Just another of our freaks. Still, she's a bright girl.

*He raps on the window affectionately, turns, and goes up the aisle.*

BORIS: By the way, I'll drive.

JAMES (*follows*): No, you won't.

BORIS: Yes, I will. I know the way, and besides I need the relaxation.

JAMES: You're not driving, Boris.

BORIS, *stopping at the door, looking back.*

BORIS: I'm sure I've forgotten to do something important.

JAMES: You're absolutely not driving, Boris.

BORIS (*shakes his head*): Ah well. It'll probably come back to me.

*He turns off the overhead lights.*

*Individual lights continue to shine from some of the cages.*

**4. Exterior. Main road, outside Oxford. Day.**

*See the car externally first. It is going very fast, then begins to slow.*

**5. Interior. Car. Main road outside Oxford. Day.**

JAMES (*watching speedometer*): More.

BORIS: Oh really, James.

*He slows a little more.*

JAMES: And keep it there, please. I really don't know why you gave up your own car.

BORIS: Probably because driving other chaps' is my version of making love to their wives. Only better. As they have to sit beside me while I do it. No, the truth is, the sods took away my licence.

JAMES (*stares at him*): You – you bloody fool! Stop the car!

BORIS: Joke, James, joke. I told you at the time why I was giving it up. For ecological reasons. Now that I've discovered I can't do without it, for sexual reasons, I've ordered a new one.

A Jap job. It does a hundred and forty. And arrives next week. If the bastards keep their promise.

JAMES: Well, you won't be driving me in it.

BORIS: I hope not. I hope I shall be driving something prettier. And more exciting. Why are you so tetchy?

JAMES: I'm not tetchy.

BORIS: How's it going with that new girlie of yours, Samantha, isn't it?

JAMES: Amanda her name is, actually.

BORIS: Samantha, Amanda, they're all the same, surely.

JAMES: No doubt to you. But not to me. As a matter of fact she's a bit fraught at the moment, she's giving her first lecture tomorrow.

BORIS: Why don't you marry her, James?

JAMES: Marry her? But I scarcely know her.

BORIS: All the better. Then there'll be a strong element of risk and it's time you took a risk. You need to shake up your pattern, James. I mean, my dear fellow, just look at you! The least sound startles you, the slightest burst of speed frightens you. In fact, I see little difference between your life and the life of one of the re-conditioned rats in my lab. Cheese, fuck, treadmill, sleep, cheese, fuck, treadmill – except in your case, there isn't much of a treadmill. Merely a leisurely ramble around a few poems. So for you it's cheese, fuck, leisurely ramble, sleep, cheese, fuck – which is why the rats are quite trim, and you're distinctly overweight, I suppose.

JAMES: I'm not in the slightest bit overweight. I've kept at thirteen one for the last two years.

BORIS: But you agree with the rest of it?

JAMES: Certainly.

BORIS: And so?

JAMES: And so nothing. What's wrong with it?

BORIS: But you're in danger of becoming a bit of a crashing bore, old chap. Look at that stupid sod!

*Honks angrily.*

*A car is overtaking on the inside. For a moment the two cars are running parallel.*

*The other car honks derisively back, then goes in front.*

I'll show the bugger!

*He puts his foot down on the accelerator and swings his car out to overtake.*

JAMES *sees a juggernaut through the window bearing down on them. He screams.*

BORIS, *who has been honking at the other car, also sees.*

Oh Christ!

*Their position looks pretty hopeless, until at the last second BORIS manages to get into a gap behind the car, which has spurted away.*

BORIS *drives on for a second or two.*

JAMES *(quietly)*: Pull over.

BORIS *pulls over to the side of the road.*

JAMES *sits blinking in shock.*

BORIS *is grinning rigidly.*

*(In a whisper.)* You nearly got us killed.

BORIS: Nonsense. My reflexes —

JAMES *leans across BORIS and opens the driving-seat door.*

JAMES: Out.

BORIS *looks at him. He sees something in JAMES's face, gets out, and walks round to the passenger side, as JAMES gets out and walks round to the driver's side. They get in.*

JAMES *(buckling himself)*: Never never

never never again, Boris.

BORIS: It's not my fault you possess a car that —

JAMES *looks at* BORIS. BORIS *stops.*

JAMES: And do up your safety-belt.

BORIS *does so.* JAMES *drives off sedately.*

BORIS: Nevertheless James, I must ask you to hurry a little. The excitement seems to have loosened my bowels. Excellent, as I've been somewhat constipated recently.

*Little pause.*

BORIS: Nevertheless, the need is urgent.

*Grins.*

JAMES *continues to drive sedately.* BORIS *gives him an anxious look. Cut to:*

## 6. Exterior. Derek's cottage. Day.

*There is a drive up to the cottage and on the other side, a lawn.*

*A vintage sports car is parked on the drive. On the lawn are a trestle table, wine in an ice bucket and scattered deck-chairs.*

DEREK, *a man of about BORIS's age, is sitting in a deck-chair, writing. He glances up as JAMES parks behind the sports car, then goes quickly back to his writing.*

BORIS *(unbuckling)*: For God's sake, James, hurry.

*He gets out of the car.* JAMES *follows.*

*We see JAMES and BORIS who is now going towards DEREK.*

DEREK *continues writing until the last minute, then puts down his board and rises.*

BORIS: Hello Derek. This is James Westgate. Fellow of Hertford, delivered as asked. James, this is Derek Newhouse, newly-elected Fellow of Magdalen.

JAMES *and* DEREK *nod at each other.*

But before we proceed further, I must beg the use of your lavatory. Where is it located?

DEREK: In the house.

*He gives a small, barking laugh.*

Ask Penny, she's in the kitchen, she'll show you.

BORIS *hurries off.*

He looks as if he's going to throw up. Is he all right?

JAMES: I think so. We had a nearish thing on the way. He's still a bit shaken, probably.

DEREK: And it scared the shit out of him, did it?

*He gives a barking laugh.*

What happened to his M.G.?

JAMES: He sold it.

DEREK: Thinks it's more exciting going about in a wheelchair does he?

JAMES: No, actually that's mine. My wheelchair.

DEREK (*barks laughter*): Wine?

JAMES: Lovely. Thank you.

DEREK *goes to the table and pours out the wine.*

DEREK: So you're at Hertford are you? What's your line?

*He gives JAMES a glass of wine.*

JAMES: English. Thank you.

*Taking the glass.*

Yours?

DEREK: Classics.

JAMES (*checking surprise*): Ah. And where were you before Magdalen?

DEREK: London. Queen Mary College. A dump down in the East End. You won't have heard of it.

JAMES: Oh, I've heard of it.

DEREK (*sits*): Really? What context?

JAMES: My father used to be one of the governors. He had a great affection for the place.

*He sits down himself. The deck-chair collapses under him. He spills his wine.*

DEREK *gives a little bark of laughter.*

DEREK: Sorry about that. My wife set them up. She's a bit cack-handed. You all right?

JAMES, *struggling up, wipes at his shirt.*

Don't worry. Only white wine. Won't stain. Although this lot tastes as if it should. Don't know where the hell she gets it from, probably the post office down in the village — try that one, it looks safe.

JAMES *lowers himself gingerly.*

DEREK *gets up with the wine bottle and brings it over.*

Here.

*He pours in more wine.*

JAMES: No, it's —

*He moves his glass away. Wine goes over his trousers.*

DEREK: Oh, sorry. It'll dry out in a second. Or eat its way through your trousers.

*He barks with laughter and stands looming over JAMES.*

It's Perks at Hertford, isn't it?

JAMES: Mmmm?

*Confused.*

DEREK: Your Principal. Perks.

JAMES: Oh. Pottsy, yes.

DEREK (*laughs*): Pottsy, is that what he's called?

JAMES: It's what I call him.

DEREK: What's he like? A bit of a prick, from what I can gather.

JAMES: I suppose he is really. But quite a — a decent one.

DEREK: Well, I've only come across him professionally. In book form. You know him well, do you?

JAMES: Yes. He's my uncle.

DEREK (*after a little pause*): Uncle?

*He gives a small bark of laughter.*

Sorry.

JAMES (*continues*): Pottsy is a family nickname. After Beatrix Potter. He used to give me one of her tales every Christmas. He still does now and then, as a matter of fact.

DEREK: Well, as I say I've never met him. In fact, I'd very much like to.

JAMES: I'm sure that won't be a problem. He's quite an accessible prick. (*He smiles.*)

DEREK: Yes, well you see, I have a slight problem over that.

JAMES: Really?

*The sound of BORIS's voice with a woman's laughter coming over it.*

DEREK *turns his head,* JAMES *follows his look, and from* JAMES's *point of view see* PENNY *and* BORIS *coming towards them. Both are carrying trays of sandwiches, coffee, another bottle of wine, strawberries, etc.*

DEREK: Oh Christ. I'll leave it until later.

*Cut to* JAMES *who is still looking at* PENNY *and* BORIS. *He is in some way clearly astonished by* PENNY. *There is an odd smile on his lips as he half-rises from his chair.*

BORIS (*meanwhile*): Yes, yes, Derek, it really is a charming little place; one expects gingerbread on the roof, and the plants to be growing chocolate buttons and other goodies.

*Putting the tray down.*

How much did you pay for it?

DEREK: Christ, Boris, you are a Wog.

BORIS: Penny, Penny (*taking her in his arms*), have I complimented you on your looks, your health, your sparkling eyes, the bloom on your cheek —

DEREK: Oh, do take your hands off her, Boris, it doesn't fool anyone.

BORIS: Penny my dear, this is James Westgate, from Hertford College; James, the ravishing Penelope, who has the misfortune to be Derek's wife.

BORIS *is leading her to* JAMES *by the hand.*

JAMES *struggles out of his chair. He is smiling intently.*

*Cut to* PENNY's *face from* JAMES's *point of view. She is taking in his expression, and looking slightly puzzled by it.*

JAMES (*holding out his hand*): How do you do?

PENNY: How do you do?

### 7.  Exterior. Derek's Cottage. Day.

*Later.* JAMES, DEREK *and* BORIS *are in deck-chairs. The sandwiches etc. have been eaten. Plates, coffee cups etc. are spread about.*

PENNY *is sitting, being observed by* JAMES. *Now and then she glances at him, as if disturbed by his scrutiny.*

PENNY: So the Marquis of whatever it was made her his mistress and bought her this house. He was absolutely bonkers about her, at least until he got her set up here, completely cut off from everybody else.

*See* DEREK *from* JAMES's *point of view, grunting without much interest.*

Then of course, after a time he simply stopped coming here, stayed on up in London and forgot about her entirely. So then *she* went absolutely bonkers —

DEREK (*interrupting*): Started screwing stable-boys, farm-hands, the bulls in the fields, anything that moved.

BORIS: Why is that bonkers? It seems an acceptable rural occupation for an out-of-work actress. For most people in fact.

PENNY: Oh, it wasn't like that at all, not at all. She merely — merely dallied with the occasional passing gentleman —

DEREK: You know who gave us all this information? Pilkington.

PENNY: No, it wasn't, darling surely. It was the people who sold it — the Merryweathers —

DEREK: No, it was Pilkington.

PENNY, *seeing* JAMES'*s eyes on her, gets up.*

PENNY: Was it? Oh, well, would anyone like another sandwich? Or strawberries or wine?

BORIS: How come Pilkington?

DEREK: Oh, he was always hanging around here. Looking for some Anglo-Saxon burial mound. In the woods at the back. Drove us mad popping in and out of the kitchen for cups of tea, prosing on about sites and measurements — Christ what a bore. And we had to go to dinner —

PENNY (*interrupting*): If everybody's finished do you mind if I clear away?

PENNY *looks towards* JAMES, *meets his eyes, looks away, and then begins to clear away plates.*

JAMES *keeps his attention on her during the following, while she is obviously avoiding his look.*

DEREK: And as for his wife, what was her name, Daphne —

PENNY: Deirdre, darling. Deirdre. Actually she's been very kind to me. Showing me all the shops —

*She comes to* JAMES *who has picked up some plates. He hands them to her.*

Thank you.

*She gives a quick smile, but avoids his glance.*

DEREK: Anyway, what's *your* theory?

BORIS: About what?

DEREK: About where he's vanished to, of course.

BORIS: Oh, it's perfectly obvious. It's just the usual mid-life crisis.

DEREK: Oh, balls, Boris!

PENNY: Thank you.

*She takes the cups, etc. from* JAMES.

JAMES *smiles at her. She gives him a quick, nervous smile, then turns away.*

DEREK: You only had to spend ten minutes in Pilkington's company to know he wasn't going through any sort of crisis, he wouldn't know what a crisis was, would he, Pen?

PENNY *has picked up a wine bottle and is pouring the last of it into some glasses. See her from* JAMES'*s point of view, still watching her from the table.*

He loves everything about his life, from being a Mediaeval historian to being short and bald with a wart on his nose. He probably even likes his lisp. And he not only dotes on his Daphne, he positively worships his two sons, he's also a children bore, isn't he, Pen?

PENNY: Actually they're daughters, darling.

DEREK: What? Yes, well the point is, he adores them, whatever they are.

BORIS: James, you know him, don't you?

JAMES: Mmmm?

BORIS: Pilkington, our vanishing don.

JAMES: Oh, Pilkington, yes. Well, only slightly. I gave a paper to that history society he runs. And went back afterwards to dinner —

BORIS: So what's your explanation?

JAMES: I haven't got one.

BORIS: Penny, some woman's wisdom please. What's happened to Pilkington?

PENNY: I really don't know, all I know is (*picking up tray*) that Deirdre and the girls miss him dreadfully, I just hope it's nothing ghastly, would anyone like some more coffee?

BORIS: There you are, Derek, as always your wife's heart has gone straight to the heart of the matter.

PENNY *turns to go.*

JAMES *is offering to take the tray.*

JAMES: Let me.

PENNY: No, it's all right, thanks.

DEREK: Yes, but the question we were discussing is not what people feel about what's happened but what's happened, and I'll tell you what's happened. He's been murdered. Oh, nothing exotic, knowing Pilkington.

JAMES: Please. I insist.

*He tries again to take the tray.*

PENNY: No, I'm all right, thank you.

DEREK: Probably picked up a hitch-hiker who bashed him over the head. Or got himself done over by a gang of hell's angels.

PENNY (*hissing*): I said I'm all right. And would you please, please, please stop staring at me, it's exceptionally rude.

*She turns with the tray and goes off with it.*

DEREK: Eventually his body'll turn up, crammed into the boot of his car, in some wasteland somewhere. Or a squad of boy scouts will tread on him in a ditch.

PENNY, *seen from JAMES's point of view is carrying the tray; still within earshot she stumbles and almost drops the tray.*

JAMES *starts, and makes to go after her but stops himself as:*

And now that that's settled, on your feet, Wog. It's time I gave you your thrashing.

PENNY, *seen from JAMES's point of view, enters the house.*

*Cut from PENNY closing the door to DEREK's face in close-up, followed by a thwack and a grunt.*

BORIS's *face in close-up is followed by a grunt and a thwack.*

DEREK's *face in close-up is followed by a grunt and thwack.*

BORIS's *face in close-up is followed by a thwack and grunt.*

*Cut to them all as seen by JAMES who is sitting in a deck-chair. They are playing badminton.*

JAMES *turns his head and looks towards the house.*

DEREK (*over*): Bloody hell, Boris. You smashed that straight at my face.

BORIS (*over*): A perfectly legitimate tactic, I believe.

DEREK (*over*): At the body. Not at the face.

BORIS (*over*): James, ruling please.

JAMES (*turning back*): I can't remember a rule against it.

DEREK *immediately serves. BORIS is not ready.*

BORIS (*retrieving*): Hah!

JAMES *turns his head and looks towards the house again.*

DEREK (*over*): What's the score?

BORIS (*over*): Yes, score, James, please.

JAMES: Um – three – one.

DEREK: Three – one! How can it be –

BORIS: Umpire's word is final, Derek.

JAMES: You'll have to get on without me for a bit, I'm afraid. I'm going in for a pee. (*Getting up.*)

BORIS: Well, hurry back. Unless you want to see blood on the lawn.

JAMES *goes towards the cottage.*

*See him in long shot approaching the house with the game in vicious progress behind him.*

### 8. Interior. The Cottage. Hall. Day.

JAMES *enters the hall. A small passage leading to a door at the end which is closed. Some stairs ahead lead to a half-landing. To the left is a door, slightly ajar.*

JAMES *hesitates, clears his throat and pushes open the door. The room is empty. It is clearly a combined sitting-room and study. There are armchairs, a sofa and bookcases with books half arranged on shelves. There is a box of books half unpacked, a desk with a typewriter on it. Books lie open on the desk along with a typescript.*

JAMES *is about to shut the door, then stops himself. He looks towards the desk, looks up the stairs and along the passageway, then slips in to the room.*

### 9. Interior. The Cottage. Study. Day.

JAMES *hurries over to the desk. He looks at the telephone, which has a pad and pencil beside it and writes the telephone's number onto the pad, rips off the page and puts it into his pocket. He hurries across the room and slips out.*

### 10. Interior. The Cottage. Hall. Day.

JAMES *looks towards the door at the end of the hall. He goes towards it, clears his throat again and listens. There is the sound of voices, low, almost muttering – a man's and a woman's.*

*He opens the door. It is the kitchen.*

### 11. Interior. The Cottage. Kitchen. Day.

*On the kitchen table is the tray from the garden. On the side of the table, a radio is on. A man and woman are discussing a piece of music. Behind the table is a door with windows. It is shut.*

JAMES *goes to the door and looks out. From his point of view we see a kitchen garden and behind it, a wood. There is a flash of movement from the wood, not distinct.*

JAMES *frowns. Peers harder. He sees nothing. He turns and goes back into the hallway, to the bottom of the stairs.*

### 12. Interior. The Cottage. Hall and stairs. Day.

JAMES *looks up, clears his throat, then walks up to the half-landing. The door is closed. He enters and closes the door. There is the sound of a lavatory flushing, a tap running etc.* JAMES *re-emerges and stands on the half-landing. He glances down then looks up the stairs. There is a door on the landing above, half-open.*

JAMES *hesitates, then goes up the stairs.*

JAMES: Hello.

*He hesitates at the door.*

Hello.

*He pushes the door open.*

### 13. Interior. The Cottage. Bedroom. Day.

*The bedroom. This is quite large, two rooms having been made into one, with a double bed.*

*There are two windows, one quite large in the corner of the room, the other smaller, adjacent to it, so that there are views of the front and side of the house.*

*Underneath the windows is a desk and on it, envelopes, writing paper, etc.*

*On either side of the bed are tables, one with an alarm clock and books, the other with books and photographs.*

JAMES *goes over to the table with the photographs. He picks them up and looks*

*t them. There is one of an elderly
couple, arms around each other. JAMES
looks at it, registers something, and puts
't down. He picks up the other
photographs.*

*He sees DEREK and PENNY in
swimming-clothes seated at a table on a
beach, PENNY with her hand on
DEREK's. JAMES looks at it with an
expression like distaste. Puts it down.*

*He goes over to the window. On the table
underneath is a framed study of DEREK
looking dramatic and handsome. JAMES
glances at it, then down at the desk.*

*On the desk is an envelope not yet sealed,
addressed to: Mrs Emily Postlethwaite,
4 The Cedars, Deal, Kent. JAMES nods
and smiles, as if confirming something to
himself.*

*JAMES glances out of the window and
from his point of view see DEREK
and BORIS having a heated altercation
over the badminton net.*

*JAMES turns, looks out of the other
window casually and see from his
point of view the figure of PENNY,
walking quickly between the trees.*

*JAMES watches for a second, then puts
the letter back in the envelope and
places it on the desk. He hurries out of
the room.*

## 14. Interior. The Cottage. Hall and Stairs. Day.

*JAMES goes downstairs to the lower
passage. He stops and looks towards the
front door, then goes into the kitchen.*

## 15. Interior. The Cottage. Kitchen. Day.

*A radio is now playing the piece of
music previously discussed.*

*JAMES goes to the door, opens it and
hurries outside.*

## 16. Exterior. The Cottage. Kitchen Garden. Day.

*JAMES is hurrying through the kitchen
garden, then hurrying towards the wood.*

## 17. Exterior. Wood behind cottage. Day.

*JAMES sees a flash of PENNY's dress
through the trees. He hurries after her. A
twig snaps underfoot. PENNY turns
quickly, looks startled, shocked, then
recognizes JAMES.*

JAMES: I'm sorry I didn't mean to – to
alarm you.

PENNY: You were following me!

JAMES: No, no, I wasn't. I was merely
wandering in this direction –

PENNY: You were following me! Just as
you were staring at me before – why?

JAMES: But I assure you, I really –
(*stops*) – you're quite right of course.
I was following you. And I was staring
at you.

PENNY: But why? Why were you?
You've made me feel quite – quite
horrid. As if you were – were after me
in some way.

JAMES: Well – because – to renew our
acquaintance. We've met before, you
see.

PENNY: Where?

JAMES: In Cornwall. In the village of
Clogmellish, in the summer of (*thinks*)
– 1961, it must have been, when I was
ten and you were eight. You don't
remember?

*PENNY shakes her head.*

I've never forgotten. Especially the
first time I saw you. I was sitting in
my room. Wondering how to get
through another sunny day. And you
appeared. Beneath my window. I'd
never seen you before, and you
shouted up, 'Well are you coming out
or aren't you?' Just like that. 'Are you
coming out or aren't you?' And I went

straight out − rather as if I'd just been sitting there waiting for you to turn up. And presented myself to you. As ordered. You looked me up and down, and you said, 'You're not up to much, from what I can see. But they say you're all there is. So you'll have to do. I suppose.' I was a bit chubby, you see. Fat, actually. And of course my glasses − anyway, off we went − on that very first day you made me do the most appalling things. Do you really not remember? When I let you down, some failure of nerve or clumsiness that messed up one of your plans, you'd assault me. Really rather violently. I've never come across such a temper. And − well, once or twice, if you were particularly tired you made me, well, put you to bed. Undress you and − tuck you up. You're the first lady I ever saw naked − and the last, for quite a few years. (*Laughs.*) And once when I was having a bath when *they* were out − actually you insisted on my having a bath, you said I smelt, you soaped me and dried me − surely you remember that?

PENNY *frowns as if in concentration.*

Look, I'm really not making this up, your real name is Prudence isn't it? Though they seem to call you Penny and Pen − ah, of course! Penelope was your second name. Right? Prudence Penelope Postlethwaite. Only you weren't Prudence or Penelope to me. Because sometimes you wore a patch over your eye − to make you look more piratical. And I had to call you Captain Patch or Patch. And you called me −

PENNY: Piglet! I remember! Of course! It's Piglet, isn't it?

JAMES: Well, Porker actually. You called me Porker.

PENNY: Of course! Porker! But I can't believe − I can't believe − but how on earth − how on earth did you recognize me? I can't possibly look the same −

JAMES: Well, that's the extraordinary thing. It wasn't you I recognized. It was the sensation. When I saw you coming across your lawn my stomach dipped. Just as it always did when I saw you coming then. In anticipation, I suppose. And a kind of − of terror. At what you had in store. That's what I recognized. The dip of my stomach. Nobody else has ever made my stomach do that. And then I recognized *you* − the nose. The eyes of course. Your um, well beauty actually. If I may say. (*Little laugh.*) The same beauty in a different form. And − the other day − about a week ago, I caught a glimpse of you − just a glimpse − on the other side of the High. And you went to a concert − at Hollywell − that would be what − two weeks ago, I suppose, wasn't it?

PENNY: Do you mind if I − if I touch you? I want to make sure you're not a − a ghost − (*Takes his hand.*) − no, no, you're flesh and you're blood, all right.

JAMES: Oh yes.

PENNY: Not a trick or a joke.

JAMES: Well, perhaps a bit of a joke. But not a trick, I don't think.

PENNY: No, you were the one person I always trusted, weren't you? That's virtually what you've been saying isn't it? You did these − these things for me − isn't that right?

JAMES: Well, I did always try −

PENNY: No, but when things were wrong. Or difficult. You see, I've been, I've been − oh, I must be careful, but I've been praying, praying frantically, just as I used to pray as a child, you know the one, Oh God, please help me, please save me, oh if you do I'll never not believe in you again − (*Stops.*) − and here you are. Piglet.

JAMES: Porker. Well, I'm not sure that I'm the answer to a prayer exactly −

but — if you need help and there's anything I can do — well, I'm yours.

*Little laugh.*

Up to a point of course.

PENNY: Up to a point?

JAMES: Well, within the usual limits.

PENNY: What limits, what are the usual limits?

JAMES: Well, of me being me. That's all I mean. I'm probably not any braver — though I'm quite a bit stronger —

PENNY: Oh, don't worry about being brave. Leave that to me. It's your help I want. That's what I need.

*They look at each other.*

JAMES: Oh good Lord, Patch. Of course I'll help you. How could I not?

PENNY *looks past him.*

JAMES *turns. See from his point of view,* DEREK *coming towards them.*

PENNY: Not fair, not fair, not bloody fair — hello, Darling, are you looking for me then?

DEREK: No, for him. (*Nodding at* JAMES.) It's all right, Boris, I've found them.

PENNY (sotto voce *to* JAMES). You've got to get in touch with me, you can't leave me in the lurch — (*to* DEREK) — but darling, you're absolutely soaking!

DEREK: Of course I'm soaking. I've been running around in the sun trying to thrash a Wog. Then running around the countryside because he's got himself into a woggish panic.

PENNY: Panic? Why's he in a panic, Darling?

DEREK: He says he's got to go back.

BORIS *appearing from further down.*

BORIS: Yes, James, sorry, I remembered what it was in the lab — it was the cat. I forgot to disconnect the bloody cat. I'll have to go straight back or I'll have

the animal rights lot ripping the place apart again.

DEREK: Oh Christ, Boris did you have to tell Penny? You know what she's like about animals.

*Both* BORIS *and* DEREK *are hot and sweaty from running.*

BORIS (*goes to her*): Ah! Sorry, Penny, my love, but anyway it's not what it sounds like.

*He puts his arm around her waist, leading her off.*

The cat was to all intents and purposes dead when it was brought to us. A very acute brain condition — not dissimilar to what is known as Alzheimer's syndrome . . .

*They are now ahead of* JAMES *and* DEREK. BORIS *is gesticulating and expostulating.* JAMES *and* DEREK *walk together.*

JAMES (*after a pause*): Your wife was showing me the woods. Very lucky to have them so close.

DEREK: Oh yes, aren't we. Apropos that conversation we were having. As our time's been cut short, I'll come straight out with it. I need a bit of help in something.

JAMES: Oh.

DEREK: Yes, with your uncle, the Principal of Hertford. Old Pottsy, as you call him.

*He gives a little bark of laughter.*

JAMES: Oh. Well, what can I do?

DEREK: This major series he's been appointed to edit. With a Channel Four link-up. It's going to be called *Mundus Antiquorum.* The point is, I need to be a part of it. At least get in on the Greek philosophers' section.

JAMES: Ah. Well, why don't you drop him a note? He really is very amenable.

DEREK: Yes, well, a few years ago, I

wrote an article dumping all over his book on Greek Tragedy. So I've got a bit of brown-nosing to do. The best thing would be to richochet off him in a social context. Oh, look out around here, by the way, Penny says she's seen an adder.

JAMES: Really? Well, they're very sensitive little creatures. As long as you don't positively step on them.

DEREK: Dinner in Hall would be best. And then back to your rooms for a quiet drink. Do you think you could arrange that?

JAMES: I'll see what I can do. Oops —

*He gives a little jump.*

no, no, only a twig.

## 18.  Exterior. The Cottage drive. Day.

BORIS *and* PENNY *are standing beside the car,* BORIS *is talking extravagantly.*

JAMES *and* DEREK *are approaching.*

BORIS (*breaking off*): Come on, James. Get a move on.

*He kisses* PENNY's *hand and gets into the car on the driving side.*

JAMES: Other side, Boris.

BORIS: If you drive we won't arrive until tomorrow.

JAMES: At least we'll arrive.

BORIS (*gets out*): Oh, thank you, Derek, for letting me give you a beating yet again.

DEREK: I don't believe all this stuff about the cat. You were beginning to fold, I'd have won the third set.

BORIS *gets in the other side,* DEREK *following him and talking through the window.*

JAMES, *during this, has gone up to* PENNY.

JAMES: Thank you for a lovely afternoon.

PENNY: Not at all.

JAMES: The next time you're in Oxford — drop in for a cup of tea or coffee. I'm in Hertford New Court. E Staircase.

*Bursts of laughter from* BORIS *and* DEREK.

PENNY (*obviously not quite hearing*): Where?

JAMES (*quickly*): New Court. E Staircase.

BORIS: Come on, James!

PENNY: I'll come tomorrow morning.

JAMES: When?

PENNY: Don't know. In the morning.

BORIS: James!

## 19.  Interior. Car. Main road outside Oxford. Day.

BORIS *and* JAMES *are travelling back to Oxford.*

BORIS: In London he was known as the ram. His real preference is for the barmaid type. By the way, he seems to have got it into his head that you're one of my lovers. Or one of my ex-lovers, possibly. He referred to you as my friend, the portly pansy.

JAMES: Did he?

*Little pause.*

Tell me, does she know?

BORIS: That he thinks you're a portly pansy?

JAMES: No, about him and his barmaids.

BORIS: Well I imagine he hopes she doesn't. After all, that must be part of the fun. Deceiving Mummy. But could we get a move on please, James?

JAMES *puts his foot down very slightly on the accelerator.*

## 20.  Interior. James's room. Night.

JAMES *is sitting on the window-seat,*

*looking out. On the gramophone we hear over, 'The Trout'.*

*Cut from* JAMES, *in the context of the room as a whole, looking out of the window, to* JAMES's *face in a trance of memory. He is smiling.*

21. Fade into montage.

**A. Concert. Day.**
*A glimpse of* PENNY *at the concert. Not properly seen.*

**B. Cottage. Day.**
PENNY *on the lawn at the cottage, smiling.*

**C. Concert. Day.**
PENNY's *face intent at the concert, listening.*

**D. Barn. Day.**
PENNY, *as a child of ten, patch over one eye, her face turned up, intent. This seen from* JAMES's *point of view on a barn roof, as he looks down. He has an elderly camera in his hands. His position is precarious.*

*Cut to* JAMES *staring down at* PENNY, *in a state of just-controlled panic.*

*Cut back to* PENNY *seen from* JAMES's *point of view. She makes an imperious gesture to* JAMES *indicating: get on with it.*

JAMES *nods, scrambles further up the barn, stops, peers down through a crack in the rafters.*

**E. Barn. Day.**
*From* JAMES's *point of view are seen a young man and woman, both in stages of undress, the girl sighing, the man heaving himself on top of her. This seen through a crack in the rafters.*

**F. Barn. Day.**
*Cut to* JAMES *staring down at them as if hypnotised. He glances down towards* PENNY.

*Cut to* PENNY, *seen from* JAMES's *point of view, staring up, as before.*

JAMES *nods, lifts the camera, makes to aim it through the crack in the rafters. Cut to:*

**G. Barn. Day.**
*Young woman's face under young man, seeming to stare straight up at* JAMES.

**H. Barn. Day.**
JAMES *losing his nerve, panicking, half turns. Camera slips from his grasp and rolls down the roof towards* PENNY.

**I. Barn. Day.**
JAMES *looking down towards* PENNY. *Her face staring up. Then through the crack, the young woman's face staring up at him in a ferocious ecstasy.*

**J. Barn. Day.**
JAMES, *now terrified, turns, slips and skids, finally topples off the barn to the ground.* PENNY *is standing over him looking down, holding the shattered camera, and cut to:*

JAMES's *and* PENNY's *point of view, both turning at a noise. Standing at the barn door is the young man, hiking up his trousers, and cut to:*

**K. Wood near barn. Day.**
JAMES *and* PENNY *running,* JAMES *limping, trailing;* PENNY *gracefully sprinting, and cut to:*

**L. Clearing in wood near barn. Day.**
JAMES *and* PENNY. JAMES *standing abjectly, sweating, spectacles dangling off his nose, chest heaving.* PENNY *standing, glaring at him.*

PENNY: Can't you do anything right? *Anything.* Anything at all! Can't you?

*She shakes the camera at him.*

JAMES: But I didn't mean to. Honestly I didn't.

PENNY: What does it matter whether you didn't mean to if you did. Oh, you're such a fool, such a fool, such a great, fat fool, Porker!

*She throws the camera at him, runs at him, pushes him to the ground aiming blows and kicks until JAMES is scrambling about blindly, spectacles broken, and cut to:*

**M. Bathroom. Day.**
JAMES *is in the bath,* PENNY *is soaping his back, and cut to:*

**N. Bedroom. Day.**
JAMES *bathed, towel around him, is undressing* PENNY. *Helping her into her pyjamas.*

JAMES *is sitting on the edge of a bed, looking down.* PENNY *is asleep.*

JAMES *takes off his spectacles, polishes the lens with the sheet as he stares down at* PENNY. *He bends over, takes the eye patch off her, bends forward and kisses her on the forehead.*

PENNY *murmurs, opens her eyes drowsily, smiles slightly, and sinks back to sleep.*

*Cut from her face, serene, to* JAMES *in college room etc.*


**22.  Interior. James's room. Night.**

*Cut back to* JAMES *in his college room, smiling as over, the sound of a telephone ringing.*

JAMES *starts, stares at the telephone uncomprehendingly, goes over to the gramophone and turns off music reluctantly. He answers the telephone.*

JAMES (*on telephone*): Hello? Oh, hello my dear, um – how are you? Good, good. What – no, no, I can't right now, my – um, the thing is I'm right in the middle of marking some essays, I've got to give them back tomorrow morning, you see, and I've spent rather a – a – fruitless afternoon out visiting some of Boris's friends – oh, ghastly, quite ghastly, and now I'm running behind so – what? What lecture? Oh,

yours, *of course* I remember, for a moment I thought you were telling me *I* was giving a lecture –

*Laughs.*

– yes, yes, no, no, I hadn't forgotten, how could I forget, your first lecture –

*Then, remembering in sudden alarm.*

but – just a minute, what time is it exactly? Oh, yes, that's fine, that's fine, I'd had some idea it was in the morning, which I couldn't have managed – my own teaching, you know.

Certainly I'll be there at three thirty on the dot, don't worry – um –

*He writes on a pad:* AMANDA. Lecture. 3.30.

– goodnight then. Goodnight.

*He puts the telephone down, goes over to the gramophone, puts on 'The Trout', goes back to the window seat, sits down and looks out. A smile returns to his face.*


**23.  Interior. James's room. Day.**

JAMES *is standing at the window, looking out impatiently for* PENNY.

*He turns into the room.*

JAMES: Um, yes. Well, we really can't go on –

*He gives a little laugh.*

– meeting like this, can we Edmund?

*Cut to* WILKINS *sitting in an armchair, a large, lumpish, intense student. His hands are folded tensely in his lap.*

After all, this is the third week running you've failed to produce an essay. Isn't it? Third week Edmund?

WILKINS *nods.*

JAMES *looks out of the window and see, from his point of view, the college courtyard.*

*He looks back at* WILKINS.

Well, what do you say?

WILKINS (*after a strangulated silence*): I don't know, sir.

JAMES: Well, look Edmund –

WILKINS (*with a ghastly grin*): Actually, it's Edward, sir.

JAMES: Mmmm?

WILKINS: Not Edmund, sir. Edward Wilkins. Edward Wilkins. Not Edmund.

JAMES: Sorry. Edward. Yes, Well – have you got a reason? For not writing me essays?

*Cut to WILKINS looking down at his hands, as if struggling to say something.*

*JAMES glances at him impatiently. Then looks out of the window. See the courtyard from his point of view.*

*A young woman wearing a straw hat is coming along the side of the court, not entirely visible but seems to be PENNY.*

*JAMES peers towards her expectantly.*

*WILKINS, over, makes an odd embarrassed noise, a kind of cough.*

*JAMES turns towards him.*

Yes, well what it comes to is this. You'd better either produce an essay or at least a plausible excuse for not doing them within the next day or so, all right?

*JAMES turns back to the window.*

*The young woman is approaching the staircase below JAMES. She lifts her face up and points, it seems, straight at JAMES.*

*An elderly American tourist joins her with a camera. He points it at JAMES.*

*Cut to JAMES's face, disappointed.*

*He turns away and discovers WILKINS staring at him intensely, as if on the point of saying something urgent.*

*JAMES looks at him, slightly puzzled,*

*lifts his hand in a farewell gesture, and turns back to the window.*

*Over, the sound of a door shutting.*

*Fade into JAMES standing at the window. Bells are tolling midday.*

*Fade into a shot of the court, JAMES staring out. Bells tolling one.*

*JAMES is sitting at the window seat, looking out. Bells are tolling two.*

*See the telephone from JAMES's point of view. Cut to the telephone and beside it a piece of paper with PENNY's number on it.*

*JAMES evidently makes a decision. He goes over to the telephone and starts to dial. His eye catches the piece of paper on which is written: AMANDA. Lecture. 3.30. He hangs up. Looks at his watch. It is 3.20 p.m. He looks towards the window in despair, then turns, and goes out.*

## 24.  Interior. Lecture hall. Day.

*JAMES goes through the main door, to the hall.*

*See AMANDA through the window of the door opposite. She is standing on a podium, reading something from a book. She is in her mid-thirties, rather plain. Other books are spread out on the lectern in front of her.*

*Cut to JAMES looking in, then back to AMANDA.*

*Students, not many, are scattered about the hall. Two of them get up and go through the door.*

*AMANDA glances desperately after them, then goes back to reading.*

FIRST STUDENT (*coming through door*): I rate that as the second most demeaning lecture I've heard this term.

SECOND STUDENT: What does she do with her voice – I mean, she can't think that's how Baudelaire's meant to sound?

*The two students pass through the main door.* JAMES *stares after them as they go out onto the street, and has a quick glimpse of* PENNY *(it certainly looks like her) cycling past. She is wearing her hat, which mostly conceals her face. (This shot is reminiscent of the shot of* PENNY *on a bicycle at the beginning of the film.) In the bicycle basket are assorted flowers, freshly cut.*

JAMES *hesitates, looks at* AMANDA *lecturing, then hurries into the street in time to see* PENNY *cycling around the corner.*

### 25.  Exterior. Streets of Oxford. Day.

JAMES *hurries along, catching occasional glimpses of* PENNY's *hat, before she turns up another street. He runs to its corner and runs along it.* PENNY *is not in sight. Suddenly he sees the bicycle, with the basket and flowers and now the hat, leaning against the wall outside a tea-room.*

JAMES *looks through the window. The shop is fairly crowded. He eventually distinguishes* PENNY, *sitting at a table by herself.*

*Cut to his face, sweaty. He is breathing heavily from running.*

*He enters the tea-room.*

### 26.  Interior. Tea-room. Day.

*In the queue for buying cakes and bread to take out, is a middle-aged woman with long, grey hair. She is not noticed by* JAMES.

JAMES *goes to* PENNY, *wiping sweat from his face with a handkerchief. Still slightly breathless. He stands looking down at her.*

JAMES: I've been waiting for you. All morning. What are you doing here?

PENNY: You gave me the wrong address. There isn't any E Staircase New Court at Magdalen.

JAMES: But I'm not at Magdalen. I'm at Hertford. Your husband's at Magdalen. And Boris is at Magdalen. I'm at Hertford.

PENNY: Oh. I suppose I just assumed – we can't talk now. I'm meant to be meeting somebody here, that's how I got away, you see, and all for nothing, all wasted. Oh God!

*She looks at him desperately.*

JAMES: I'm meant to be meeting somebody too. But afterwards –

PENNY: No, I've got to go back. Almost immediately. Derek needs the car, you see. I can't be late.

JAMES: Oh.

*Then realising.*

The car? But you haven't got the car – you're on a bicycle.

PENNY: Bicycle?

*She looks beyond* JAMES, *sees someone and smiles.*

JAMES *turns, as a distraught woman in her middle thirties appears and sits down, unaware of* JAMES.

DEIRDRE (*to* PENNY): I'm sorry I'm late. Especially after summoning you out like this. But I desperately needed – need – to talk. I – I –

*She fumbles in her bag and takes out a cigarette. Hand trembling, she lights it and puffs on it.*

– I'd given them up. But this last week –

DEIRDRE *gives a little laugh, fraught, she suddenly takes in* JAMES.

– sorry, I interrupted you.

PENNY: No, no, we just bumped into each other –

*She looks at* DEIRDRE *with concern.*

DEIRDRE: But we've met, haven't we? You're James Westgate. You came to dinner once. About a year ago.

JAMES: Oh – um –

*Not placing her.*

DEIRDRE: After you'd given a paper for my husband's history thing — I'm Deirdre Pilkington.

JAMES: Oh. Oh yes. Yes.

DEIRDRE: I don't know what your views are — everybody has a view, I know, including, I gather, that he was on the verge of being unmasked as an embezzler, and there are even a couple of scatty — no, not scatty, *vicious* girls going around claiming — although why they think that's a reason for him to run away from his home and his work — I mean, if they were telling the truth he could scarcely be better off, could he, with lots of nubile students and a completely unsuspecting wife —

*She gives a little laugh.*

— but the fact is, whatever your particular view, he's dead. Murdered. (*This said defiantly.*)

PENNY: Oh Deirdre! (*Upset.*) Don't —

DEIRDRE: Now all they've got to do is find a shred of evidence. His body, for instance. But to do that, they'll have to start looking seriously for him, won't they?

*All this is said to* JAMES. *He stands, smiling meaninglessly.*

Sorry, sorry, my dear.

*To* PENNY.

But I've just come from the police, you see. I told myself I wasn't going to go today, but I had to pass the station to get here, and found myself dropping in — and the dreadful man behind the desk, just like that one who used to be on television years back, the 'hello, hello, hello' one, pretending to be so avuncular but all the time I could tell what *his* real view was, his particular view, that I'm a sad but tiresome middle-aged woman who can't accept the obvious, that her husband's abandoned her from boredom or run off with his floozy,

and it's really all my own fault for not knowing how to keep him at home. Nobody — nobody in the world — except me and his children seems to understand that he was a nice man — a good man. Who loves us actually. And would never — never just abandon us. (*To* PENNY.) Of course you understand, Penny. I do know that. Sorry, my dear.

DEIRDRE *puts her hand on* PENNY'*s. Both women are upset.*

JAMES: I — I can't say how sorry, how very sorry um — well, I'd better leave you — oh, may I just ask, what time is Derek leaving, I mean if I went out now would I catch him — excuse me? (*To* DEIRDRE.)

PENNY: He's going at four-thirty promptly, I'm terribly sorry, Deirdre, that's when I've got to get back — because of the car, you see.

DEIRDRE: It's my own fault, for being late.

PENNY: So if you're after four-thirty you'll miss him completely. But he probably won't be gone too long — probably not more than an hour or so. And then he'll be back.

JAMES: Right. I've got that.

JAMES *looks at* DEIRDRE *blankly.*

Well, nice to have met you.

*With a smile, he turns and goes. Turns as he leaves and nods to* PENNY *then goes out into the street.*

**27.  Exterior. The tea-room. Day.**

*Through the window, from* JAMES'*s point of view see* PENNY *still leaning forward and* DEIRDRE *wiping her eyes with a handkerchief.*

JAMES *stands for a moment, then turns as the middle-aged woman with long, grey hair from the queue comes out of the shop. She has rather a ravaged face. She is*

*holding a box of cakes. She goes to the
bicycle, puts the box in the basket beside
the flowers, pushes her hair on her head,
puts on her hat, and cycles off.*

*As she recedes, the image becomes like*
PENNY *again.*

JAMES *stares after her, then turns and
walks slowly down the street. He
suddenly stops in realisation, looks at his
watch and hurries off, almost running.*

### 28.  Interior. Lecture Room. Day.

JAMES *hurries in, panting and sweating.
He goes to the lecture room. Looks
through the window. It appears to be
empty. He looks around, then looks
through the window of the lecture room
again. He sees* AMANDA *sitting, hunched
in a corner, smoking.*

*He enters the lecture room.*

### 29.  Interior. Lecture Room. Day.

AMANDA *looks up at* JAMES *and
attempts a smile.*

*He goes over to her.*

JAMES: Sorry I'm late, the thing is —
(*checks himself*) — how did it go?

AMANDA: Oh James, it was awful. They
left in droves and then when I started
reading Baudelaire something happened
to my throat, nerves I suppose, I
sounded just like Donald Duck. At
least from the inside, I expect I did
from the outside too.

*She looks at him. Her mouth trembles.
She is clearly on the verge of tears.*

Well, let's be off to somewhere I can
feel invisible for a time. (*Gets up.*)

JAMES: Yes, well the awful thing is I've
got to go.

AMANDA: Oh.

JAMES: You see, it's my father. I've just
heard he's very ill, very ill indeed, so
I've got to go to London, he's in
hospital.

AMANDA: Oh James, I am so sorry and
here I've been wingeing on about a
silly lecture.

JAMES: Look, we'll have dinner. I'll take
you to the French place.

AMANDA: You won't be back in time.
Come straight to me and I'll cook us
something.

JAMES: Right. Thank you.

*He bends forward and kisses her.*

AMANDA *puts her arms around him.*

AMANDA: Oh James, I am sorry.

JAMES: Well, um, see you later then.

*He hurries to the door and glances
through the window. See* AMANDA
*from his point of view. He gives her
a little wave.*

### 30.  Interior/Exterior. Car. End of
### Derek's drive. Day.

JAMES *is sitting in his car parked by the
side of the road off* DEREK's *drive. He
looks at his watch. It is 4.35.*

*There is the sound of the sports car
coming up the drive.*

JAMES *ducks his head as* DEREK *comes
up the drive and turns towards the main
road. He watches it as it gets to the
turning. It is coughing slightly but goes
around the corner.*

JAMES *drives his car down the drive.*

### 31.  Exterior. Derek's Cottage. Day.

*As* JAMES *approaches the cottage, the
door opens.* PENNY *comes out, walking
very quickly, almost running towards
him. He gets out of the car.*

PENNY (*anxiously*): Did Derek see you?

JAMES: No, no, it's all right. I waited
around the corner. He went past me
without a glance.

*There is a roaring sound from the
drive.* JAMES *and* PENNY *turn
towards the noise and from their*

*point of view, see* DEREK *coming back down the drive. Just before he gets to the house, the car jumps a bit, then stalls.*

DEREK *gets out, furious.*

DEREK: You forgot to get the petrol. I asked you to fill her up in Oxford. I reminded you just before you left. If I hadn't noticed, I'd have been stuck on the bloody bypass.

PENNY: Oh darling, I'm so sorry. So sorry. It went straight out of my mind. Because of Deirdre being so upset and —

DEREK: Bugger Deirdre, you were late getting back anyway. What am I going to do, I've got a seminar in twenty minutes time, post-graduates —

PENNY: I'll 'phone for a taxi.

DEREK: You know how I hate wasting money on taxis. Besides, it'll take them half an hour to get here —

*He sees* JAMES.

### 32. Interior. James's car. Main road outside Oxford. Day.

DEREK *and* JAMES *are in the car.* JAMES *is driving,* DEREK *beside him. There is silence between them. During the course of the journey* DEREK *is only just suppressing irritation with* JAMES's *careful driving.*

DEREK (*after a moment*): Very good of you.

JAMES: Not at all. I was on my way back anyway.

DEREK: Where from?

JAMES: Mmmm?

DEREK: Where were you on your way back from?

JAMES: Oh. Visiting my father. He's in hospital.

DEREK: He lives around here, does he?

JAMES: No. In London, as a matter of fact.

DEREK: Rather a long way around.

JAMES: Mmmm?

DEREK: Coming from London.

JAMES: Yes. I like to go by the side-roads. A whiff of the country —

DEREK, *paying no attention, glances at the speedometer.*

DEREK: Anything serious?

JAMES: Mmmm?

DEREK: Your father.

JAMES: Oh, it is rather, I'm afraid. Yes. What's the seminar on?

DEREK: Plato. *The Symposium.*

JAMES: Ah. The Greek ideal of love, eh?

DEREK: That's the ticket. (*Looking at his watch.*)

JAMES: I re-read it often. The school chaplain introduced me to it. He was a great teacher, and an exceptionally sensitive and feeling man. Especially with boys of my age.

DEREK *glances sardonically at* JAMES *and grunts.*

I mean boys of my age the age I was then. (*Little laugh.*) Sixteen. He'd have little seminars — well, symposiums, he actually called them — with the two or three lads in whom he took a special interest.

DEREK *throws him a contemptuous glance.*

Really, it was because of him, and through him because of Plato . . .

### 33. Exterior. Magdalen College. Day.

JAMES *pulls up beside it.*

JAMES: There you are, and not even late.

DEREK: Thanks. You saved my bacon. Now the question is how the hell am I going to get back? Look, what are you up to this evening?

JAMES (*stares at* DEREK): Well, um, nothing.

JAMES *gives a little laugh.*

DEREK: Good. Then why don't you pick me up here at 7.30.

JAMES: Oh, right.

DEREK: You can come and have a bite of supper with us or something.

JAMES: Thank you.

DEREK *wags his hand as he turns to go.*

JAMES *wags his hand.*

### 34. Exterior. Main road outside Oxford. Day.

JAMES *is driving his car back to the cottage.*

### 35. Exterior. End of Derek's drive. Day.

JAMES *goes down the drive.*

### 36. Interior. Derek's cottage. Hall. Front door. Day.

*The door is ajar.* JAMES *pushes it open and see from his point of view down the length of the corridor into the kitchen.*

PENNY *is sitting at the kitchen table, her cheek resting on her hand. The radio is on. Mozart playing. She is softly lit by light from the kitchen windows. The effect is almost religious.*

JAMES *stands looking, in wonder.*

PENNY *looks up.*

### 37. Interior. The Cottage. Kitchen. Day.

*From* PENNY'*s point of view* JAMES'*s figure is indistinct. She stares for a second, then screams hysterically, getting up. She continues to scream, close to hysteria.*

JAMES *runs to her, grabs her as she continues to scream, and puts his arms around her.*

JAMES: It's only me, it's only me.

PENNY *collapses within his arms.* JAMES *strokes her hair with an expression of tender concern on his face.*

Only me, Patch, only me, only me.

### 38. Interior. The Cottage. Kitchen. Day.

JAMES *and* PENNY *sit at the kitchen table in silence.* JAMES *has his hand on hers.*

PENNY: Can I really trust you? Really?

JAMES: You lead, I'll follow – that's what you used to say, when we were setting out on one of your escapades.

PENNY: But this isn't an escapade, you see. It's a nightmare. And today you've been part of it, turning up when I was meeting Deirdre, of all people, then driving up, and driving straight off with Derek, then Derek 'phoning up saying you were coming back with him, then standing at the door looking just like – like – with your glasses glinting – just more out of the nightmare.

JAMES: Here, feel –

*He squeezes her hand and raises it to his cheek.*

– still flesh and blood, just as I was yesterday. And I'm here in spite of everything. Now tell me what the matter is, Patch. Is it – (*hesitates*) – is it Derek?

PENNY *looks at him.*

Something wrong between you and Derek?

PENNY: No, no, it isn't him. Well, of course it is in a way. Because he's the whole point. Whatever happens he musn't know, you see. Musn't.

JAMES: I've already promised I won't tell a soul. (*Then swallowing.*) It's another man then, perhaps, is it?

PENNY: You might put it that way, yes. Another man.

## 39. Exterior. Ditch in woods. Day.

*See* PILKINGTON's *face, glasses down over his nose, eyes open, scissors sticking through his neck. See this from* JAMES's *point of view, then the camera travels along to take in the whole body, bits of leaves and twigs scattered over it.*

*Cut to* JAMES's *face, looking down.*

PENNY, *beside him, watches him. After a long pause:*

PENNY: Look at his glasses. See how they glint!

JAMES: Yes. Who is it exactly?

PENNY: Horace.

JAMES: Horace. Um, Horace who?

PENNY: Pilkington.

JAMES: Ah. What — what exactly happened to him, then?

PENNY: I killed him, you see. So there you are, Piglet. Your little chum Patch has grown up into a murderess.

JAMES (*nods*): Do you mind if we go and sit somewhere, I feel a trifle —

## 40. Exterior. A wall near the woods. Day.

JAMES *and* PENNY *sit on the wall.* JAMES *stares straight ahead.* PENNY *watches him anxiously.*

PENNY: You're not going to let me down now, are you? After all you've promised?

JAMES: Um — well how did it happen precisely?

PENNY: I told you. I killed him.

JAMES: Yes, but it must have been a sort of — sort of accident, mustn't it? I mean you didn't just — just stick those things into him on a whim, I take it. (*Little laugh.*) Did you?

PENNY: No, no, of course not. I stuck them into him on purpose.

JAMES: What was the purpose, Patch?

PENNY: To stop him, of course. You see, he came over — when Derek was in London, seeing his publisher — and was messing about in the woods, looking for his precious burial mound or whatever it was he was always looking for. And I was reading on the lawn and he suddenly came gambolling up — saying he'd found it, he was sure he'd found it at last, come and look, please Penny. So I went — I — I'd much rather not go through it all again, Piglet.

JAMES: I think I really need to know, Patch.

JAMES *looks at her.*

PENNY (*after a pause*): Oh, all right then. Well, where was I?

JAMES: He was showing you the burial mound.

PENNY: Yes. (*Pause.*) And then he began. That's when it happened, you see.

JAMES: Began what?

PENNY: To touch me. He was everywhere. His hands, I mean, they were everywhere. Under my skirt and on my breasts and his spectacles — and his spectacles were butting against my face, and then I saw his scissors. I picked them up and just — just stuck them in him.

JAMES: What did you do then, Patch?

PENNY: Went in and had a bath, of course. I was covered with blood.

JAMES: And then?

PENNY: I sat in the kitchen, waiting for Derek. Thinking about how to tell him. Tell him what I'd done to Horace.

JAMES: Why didn't you?

PENNY: Oh, I tried to once or twice but it was impossible. Quite impossible. When he got home he was in such a state because his book had been turned down by the publishers, you see. On Socrates, Man and something

— myth — myth. So of course that's what he wanted to talk about and I had to keep saying how disgusting, how disgraceful, how shameful and shocking as he went over and over what they'd said to him and he'd said to them. Then I heated up some soup, we went through it all again and then we went to bed.

*She looks at* JAMES.

That's all, really. So what should we do, Piglet?

**41. Interior. The Cottage. Kitchen. Day.**

JAMES *pours himself a large scotch. His hand trembles.* PENNY *watches him anxiously.*

JAMES (*after a long pause*): But surely, if you told it to them just as you've told it to me . . .

PENNY: Yes, but you see, think of the publicity. The trial. There'd certainly have to be a trial, wouldn't there?

JAMES *nods.*

I might even go to jail, mightn't I?

JAMES: Oh, I don't think — I'm sure that — after all, he assaulted you.

PENNY: Oh, it's not my going to jail, but what it would do to Derek, even if I didn't. He's only just come to Oxford, it would be talked about in the College, among his students, everywhere. He couldn't endure that. He'd hate me for it.

JAMES: Yes. I see. (*Clears his throat.*) I take your point but — I can't help feeling that the proper course, in the long run —

PENNY *looks at* JAMES *and smiles bitterly.*

PENNY: You're going to tell them, aren't you? Derek and the Police.

JAMES: No. No, of course not. (*Pause.*) But if you — we — *we* don't do the normal thing — *proper* thing — legal

thing, that is — you can't leave him where he is, can you?

PENNY: Of course not. That's what I want you to help me with.

JAMES (*after a slight pause*): Yes.

DEREK *enters.*

PENNY: Darling! You're back. How lovely!

JAMES *assumes beaming nonchalance.*

JAMES: Oh, hello there. Um. Derek —

DEREK *gives a little bark of angry laughter as he stares at* JAMES.

DEREK: What happened to you then?

JAMES: Mmmm?

DEREK: You were going to pick me up at half-past-seven.

JAMES: Oh Lord! (*Slaps his forehead.*) Derek, I'm terribly sorry, I suppose — I suppose that with one thing and another you completely slipped my mind.

DEREK *gives a short bark of incredulous laughter.*

You see, I had to chair the wine committee, and it ran over a bit. Because of the port. I am sorry. How did you get back?

DEREK: By bloody taxi.

*He attempts a slightly more jocular tone.*

I slipped your mind too, did I?

PENNY: What?

DEREK: Well, I did 'phone and tell you he'd be picking me up. Didn't you notice I wasn't here?

PENNY: But he's only just arrived, darling. I thought you were together. Or just behind him, rather. What you need is a drink.

*She sees the scotch bottle and glass on the table, and picks them up smoothly.*

I was just about to pour one for Piglet.

DEREK: Piglet?

JAMES: Actually it's Porker, my — my friends call me Porker, as I was just in the middle of explaining to — um — Pa — Patch — (*checking himself*) — Prudence. Thank you. (*Receiving drink.*)

DEREK: Prudence? (*Looks at* PENNY.)

PENNY: Yes, well I was explaining that my real name was Prudence, though my friends call me Penny or Pen.

DEREK: In my case we'll settle for Derek, can we?

JAMES *and* PENNY *laugh.*

JAMES: Well, I'll drink to that. (*Catches* PENNY'*s eye.*) How did the seminar go?

## 42. Interior. The Cottage. Kitchen. Night.

DEREK, JAMES *and* PENNY *sit around the kitchen table.* DEREK *is at the head,* JAMES *and* PENNY *opposite each other. They eat dinner.* PENNY *is talking with too much animation to* DEREK.

PENNY: . . . when I told him he'd actually taken the measurements down himself, because I remembered his name, it was Parker, (*small hesitation*) he said, do you know what he said, darling, he said, 'Oh well, I must have mislaid them!'

JAMES: How infuriating! But there's another place, you know, just around the corner from Hubblewickes called Fabrics and Frolics, I think it is. Some such name anyway. I went there with a friend's wife when she was doing up their flat, and they really do have some very charming patterns.

DEREK *glances at* JAMES *contemptuously.*

PENNY: Just around the corner from Hubblewickes, you say, oh, I must go

and have a look.

DEREK: Did you remember to call the garage?

PENNY: The garage?

DEREK: Yes, the garage. To get them to bring some petrol over. To save me hiking up there in the morning.

PENNY: Oh darling, I'm terribly sorry. I can't think why —

DEREK: It probably just slipped your mind, eh?

PENNY: Sorry.

*They eat in silence for a moment.*

(*Desperately.*) Oh, that reminds me, somebody 'phoned. Now, who did she say she was — oh, oh — oh, that's right, Liz Maybrick.

DEREK: Who?

PENNY: Liz Maybrick, one of your research students from London, she said she was.

DEREK: Oh. Oh yes. What did she want?

PENNY: Only to tell you that they've taken away her grant and could you 'phone her back.

DEREK: Grant? (*A moment's pause.*) Taken it away, eh? I'm not surprised. Utterly chaotic little mind. I warned her they would.

PENNY: Actually, I did say you'd call her back as soon as you got in. She said you had her number.

DEREK: I expect I have, somewhere at College. So she'll have to wait until tomorrow.

*A pause.*

Oh, by the way, I was right about Pilkington, he's been murdered.

*A silence.*

JAMES: Indeed? How do you know?

DEREK: College porter told me. Police found his car. Just up the road in Little Mitford. Some woman's been complaining all week about it's having been parked outside her house, in her spot, so this morning they got around to having a look at it. (*Bark of laughter.*) So much for Boris and the mid-life crisis. But it's bad news for you, Pen. (*To* PENNY.) You can expect them around any time.

PENNY *is frozen.*

JAMES: How exciting – this is delicious, by the way.

PENNY: Thank you, I'm sorry it's only frozen. (*Then somewhat restored.*) Why do you think they'll come here, darling?

DEREK: Because Pilkington used to hang about here, of course, and Little Mitford's walking distance. So they're bound to come trampling over the lawn, thundering through the woods, and dragging through the ditches.

JAMES (*seeing* PENNY'*s face*): But tell me why exactly, exactly why finding the car means he was murdered, Derek. Doesn't altogether follow surely, I'm speaking on behalf of Boris, of course, and the mid-life theory. (*Little laugh.*)

DEREK: Because the keys were in the ignition. So either somebody drove it there and left it in a panic, or Pilkington got out with every intention of coming back. So what would your Boris have to say to that little lot?

JAMES: Well, well I suppose he might say –

*The telephone rings.*

DEREK (*quickly*): I'll get it.

*He goes out. Pause.*

JAMES: You didn't tell me about the car.

PENNY: He used to park it at the top of the drive. I couldn't just leave it there, could I?

JAMES: Yes, but – um – why did you leave it so close? Within walking distance he said.

PENNY: Becuase I had to walk back.

JAMES: Ah. And you left the keys in the ignition.

PENNY: Because I hoped someone would steal it. There's no point in telling me I've done everything wrong, I know I have, I know it. The question is what are we going to do now?

JAMES: Yes, well it's obvious that whatever it is, we're going to have to do it straight away.

PENNY: Tomorrow. You've got to do it tomorrow.

JAMES: What time does Derek go out?

PENNY: He doesn't. He works at home on Thursdays.

JAMES: Can you get him out? In the evenings? Or at night, would be best. More conventional, too, I'd think. For burying bodies on the quiet. (*Little laugh.*)

PENNY *gives him a look.*

Sorry.

*Sound of* DEREK *returning.*

PENNY: And for God's sake, stop him talking about it.

DEREK *enters, trying to look casual.*

DEREK: Sorry, wrong number. But the fool wouldn't believe me. Seemed to think I was a pub or something. (*Sitting down.*) Yes, now you were just about to give us the Boris line on Pilkington, I believe.

JAMES: Was I? Well I don't know what it would be, even Boris would be a bit floored by the car business. A pub, eh? That's unusual. To be mistaken for a pub. Which one did he think you were?

DEREK: Oh, (*desperately*) The Cat's Whiskers, I think it was, yes. The Cat's Whiskers. Oh, and another thing about Pilkington's car –

JAMES: I don't believe I've ever come across a pub called The Cat's Whiskers before, have you? (*To* PENNY.)

PENNY: Not The Cat's Whiskers, no. Never.

JAMES: Was it a man or a woman?

DEREK: Man, why, what's that got to do with it?

JAMES: Oh I was just sort of curious. What sort of accent?

DEREK: Accent?

JAMES: Yes. Did he sound like a local chap or —

DEREK: No idea, I suppose he sounded a bit — bit North Country, anyway, it doesn't matter, what I'd like to ask the police —

JAMES: North Country! Now that *is* interesting. Because of these new dialling codes, you see. They're so complicated that if someone wanted, say, a pub called The Cat's Whiskers in Leeds he'd only have to get one digit wrong to find himself asking if you were The Cat's Whiskers here in Oxford. Although I admit that doesn't settle the question as to whether you'd be likely to be The Cat's Whiskers anywhere, in fact, the Cat's anything . . . I mean, not only have I never come across The Cat's Whiskers . . . The Cat's Pyjamas, for instance, I don't believe I've ever come across The Cat's Cradle, The Cat on the Mat, The Cat and Dog — The Cat —

DEREK (*interrupting*): Well, I assure you that's what she said. The Cat's Pyjamas. (*Slight pause.*) Cat's Whiskers, that is.

JAMES: She said?

DEREK: What?

JAMES: You said she said. But before you said —

DEREK: I meant he. He said. I must say — I must say — I'd really like to get back to the topic of the moment, if you don't mind. Which happens to be the scissors.

JAMES: Scissors?

DEREK: Pilkington's scissors. The ones he used to cut up his tape with. Now what I'd ask the police, if I could be bothered, was whether the scissors were in the car. Because if they *weren't* in the car —

PENNY *lets out a moan.*

Something the matter?

PENNY: Just — just a headache.

DEREK: What, another one? (*Gets up.*) I'll get you an aspirin. That makes one almost every evening for the last week or so, if it keeps up you'll *have* to see a doctor, Pen.

*He goes to the tap and pours a glass of water.*

PENNY *grabs* JAMES's *hand, clutches at it, then relinquishes it as* DEREK *turns.*

PENNY *takes the aspirin and drinks the water.*

PENNY: I think — if you don't mind — I think I'd better go and lie down.

*She gets up.*

DEREK: Won't do you much good unless you turn the lights off. She's taken to trying to sleep with the light on.

PENNY (*to* JAMES): I'm sorry to abandon you —

JAMES: Not at all. You get some rest.

PENNY *smiles, then nods. As she goes out she turns and stares at* JAMES, *pleadingly.*

JAMES *gives her a little nod of encouragement.*

PENNY *closes the door.*

DEREK: Never used to have them in London. Must be the country air.

*He hesitates, and attempts a smile.*

By the way, all that stuff about the cat's what's it and pubs, what was that all about?

JAMES: Sorry?

DEREK: Well, you gave the impression you were trying to tell me something. Or Penny something. Or something.

JAMES: Really? What sort of something?

DEREK: I don't know. That's what I'm asking you.

JAMES: No, I assure you – I've always had a great interest in the derivation of things like pubs' names, in fact I once wrote a little paper –

DEREK: Oh, I see. That's all right then. I just don't want Penny to be worried about anything, you see. What with all these headaches and bad nights she's been having. So I don't want her worried, that's all.

JAMES: Of course, I'll be very careful.

DEREK: Right. That's understood then.

*A pause.*

JAMES: Well, er, I'd better be off then. Leave you to look after my wife – (*little laugh*) – your wife, I mean.

DEREK: Well, perhaps I'd better make sure she's put herself to bed.

*They go into the hall.*

### 43.  Interior. The Cottage. Hall. Night.

JAMES: Thank her for dinner for me. (*Turning to go.*) I hope her head clears up – um – oh –

*As he opens the front door.*

oh, something, *yes of course*! (*Slaps his forehead.*) How could I have forgotten – old Pottsy, I saw him this evening – at the wine committee. Now the thing is, he's off to the States for a couple of months, leaves on Saturday. To recruit contributors for the series.

DEREK: Well, that cuts me out, doesn't it? Bugger! Bugger the Americans!

JAMES: Ah, well all isn't quite lost. He's going to be in Hall tomorrow night, why don't you come to dinner and I'll find some way of bringing you two together?

DEREK: Right. That's very good of you. Thanks.

JAMES: Good. I'm in New Court. The porter will show you where, so see you in my rooms at 7.30.

DEREK: I'll be there.

*JAMES turns to go, then turns back.*

JAMES: Look, why don't you stay the night in College?

DEREK: Why?

JAMES: Well, um, you know what it's like, one tends to drink rather a lot in Hall on these occasions. And you see a few years ago some chap I invited, well, rather a tragedy, he didn't make it home. I'm afraid. In fact he's virtually a vegetable.

DEREK (*little laugh*): Really, Well don't worry about me, I can keep an eye on myself, thanks.

JAMES: Oh. Right. Well, do you mind if I reserve a guest room just in case you change your mind?

DEREK: If you want to (*little laugh*) but I doubt if I'll be using it.

JAMES: See you tomorrow then.

*JAMES wags his hand, and goes out.*

### 44.  Exterior. The Cottage. Drive. Night.

DEREK *wags his hand.*

JAMES *goes to his car and gets in.*

DEREK *wags his hand again.* JAMES *wags his back as he drives off.*

*See* DEREK *from* JAMES's *point of view, closing the door. Stay with* JAMES *going up the drive. He stops the car. Gets out, and comes quietly back down the drive. He sees* DEREK *framed at the sitting-room window, as he draws the curtains.*

JAMES *steals closer and looks through a slight gap in the curtains.* DEREK *is standing in a state of indecision. He looks up at the ceiling, looks at his watch, then goes to the telephone and dials.*

JAMES *bends down, picks up a handful of gravel and throws it against the window above.*

*Silence.*

JAMES (*urgently, in a low voice*): Patch! Patch! Patch!

*Silence.*

*He looks through the curtain again. DEREK is talking on the telephone.*

JAMES *picks up more gravel and throws it against the window.*

*From inside PENNY's room comes a shriek of terror.*

*Cut to JAMES's face, appalled. He glances through the curtains.*

DEREK *glances, puzzled, up at the ceiling, waits for a second, then goes on talking on the telephone.*

JAMES *looks up at the window above.*

PENNY *opens the curtains and stares down at him, terrified.*

JAMES *steps back a bit so she can see him properly. She recognises him, pushes the window open wider and leans out.*

PENNY: What are you doing? You frightened me nearly to death.

JAMES: Sorry.

*He glances through the window to make sure DEREK is still on the telephone.*

Listen, we'll do it tomorrow. I'll be coming out around midnight. I'll phone you just before I leave.

PENNY: What about Derek?

JAMES: Don't worry, I'm working that out, but he's coming to dinner tomorrow with me. You try and persuade him to spend the night at my College. Because of drinking and driving and so forth. Have you got that?

*He glances through the window again.*

*He sees DEREK still on the telephone.*

PENNY: He won't.

JAMES: Well try anyway. But don't worry, I'll find a way of keeping him there. Everything's going to be all right.

PENNY: Do you promise?

JAMES: I promise.

JAMES *glances through the window, and sees DEREK has left the room.*

Don't forget I'll phone you.

DEREK (*over*): What are you doing? You're meant to be in bed.

PENNY (*withdrawing from window*): Oh, just getting – getting some fresh air.

DEREK *comes to the window. We have just a glimpse of him standing beside PENNY as she draws the curtains. The sound of their voices is no longer audible as JAMES looks once at the window, then turns.*

## 46. Interior. James's rooms. Morning.

*The camera comes straight in on a writing pad. 'Hall' and 'Guestroom' have been ticked off.*

*Cut to JAMES on the telephone.*

JAMES (*on telephone*): Master, please. Oh hello, Potts. Nutkin. Just wondering whether you're going to be in Hall tonight. Oh, good, because there's somebody who's frantically keen to meet you. Oh, his name is – um Derek Newhouse, actually. Yes, that's right, Derek Newhouse. (*Little pause.*) Oh, I see. I'd no idea. Wrote what! Good Lord! I'd have thought that's libellous. Oh dear, well listen Potts, I promise I won't inflict him on you for more than a few minutes, over the port, would you mind, be as rude to him as you like, you see I did promise and perhaps he wants to apologise, eh? Oh come on Potts, just a very little nut for Nutkin. Thanks. (*Hangs up.*)

*He ticks off* 'POTTS' *on the list, then hesitates a moment before starting to dial once more.*

(*Dials.*) Hello. I wonder if I could speak to Doctor Ramsay. (*Pause.*)

James Westgate of Hertford College, I'm one of her patients. (*Little pause.*) Well it's just that I need a prescription for sleeping pills. I see. Well could she give me a ring the moment she's free?

*There is a knock at the door.*

(*Abstractedly.*) Come in.

WILKINS *walks in, knotted with feeling.*

JAMES: Right, thank you. (*Puts down phone.*) (*Looks at him.*) Yes?

WILKINS: You told me to come and see you.

JAMES: Did I? About what?

WILKINS: Well – um – to give you an essay or my excuse.

*He comes into the room a bit more.*

And I've – um – come to give you my excuse.

JAMES: Oh right. Fire away.

WILKINS: The thing is I'm in love. Hopelessly in love. That's my excuse – er – James.

JAMES: Really? Well, don't worry about it. It happens to all of us, so –

WILKINS: But it's a question – of who – who I'm in love with.

JAMES: Well, I suppose it does make a difference but the thing is – look – Ed – um – Ed – um – I've got rather a busy day. Perhaps this isn't the time – for one thing I'm waiting for the doctor to –

WILKINS (*blurts out*): It's you James.

JAMES: What?

WILKINS: It's you I'm in love with.

JAMES: Ah.

WILKINS: I have been since our first

supervision. It's paralysed me. That's why I haven't been able to do a shred of work. I'm terrified of your judgement on me.

JAMES: Well, that explains everything, Ed – um.

WILKINS: What do you mean, James?

JAMES: I mean – well, excuse accepted. Quite all right. I understand. You can go.

WILKINS: Go?

AMANDA (*appears at the door*): Oh, sorry. I didn't realise.

*She is clearly in an emotional state.*

WILKINS *stares yearningly at* JAMES, *smoulderingly at* AMANDA, *turns, and goes out.*

AMANDA (*looking after* WILKINS): Have I come at a bad time?

JAMES: Well – (*gives a little laugh*).

AMANDA: I just wanted to know how he was.

JAMES: Who?

AMANDA: Your father.

JAMES: Oh – um – much better, much better than everyone seemed to think.

AMANDA: Good. I was a bit worried, you see, as you were going to come straight to me from the hospital. So of course I assumed something rather serious must have happened.

JAMES: Oh, God, I'm terribly sorry, I completely forgot. You see, I suddenly remembered I had a wine committee meeting last night. I got back just in time for it.

AMANDA: A wine committee meeting?

JAMES: Yes, it was interminable. A question of whether to buy some port or wait until a better year came up for auction. It all got rather fractious, you know how these things go, and by the time we'd finished it would have been far too late to – er – disturb you anyway.

AMANDA: Well, did you or didn't you?

JAMES: What?

AMANDA: Buy the port.

JAMES: Ah, no. Final vote went against. Twelve ten, I think it was.

AMANDA: You mean there were twenty-two people on the wine committee?

JAMES, *in spite of himself, lets out a little laugh.*

AMANDA: There wasn't a wine committee, was there?

JAMES, *about to protest, decides against.*

JAMES: No.

AMANDA: In other words, you just didn't want to see me, did you?

JAMES *looks at her. The telephone rings.*

JAMES (*picking up telephone*): Hello? Yes, that's right, speaking. Doctor who? (*Pause.*) No, it was Doctor Ramsay I wanted to speak to. (*Pause.*) What? Oh, oh I see. I see. Yes, of course. I'll come straight away.

*He puts the telephone down and looks at* AMANDA.

Sorry, I can't – I can't – that was a doctor. I've got to dash you see. Up to London.

*Cut to* AMANDA's *face, then back to* JAMES.

Apparently it's my father.

## 47. Interior. Hospital corridor outside private room. Day.

*From* JAMES's *point of view, with a doctor standing beside him, we look through a window in a door. A robust, elderly man sits up in bed, and writes furiously on a typewriter on a board across the bed. He throws back his head and laughs.*

JAMES: That's not my father.

DOCTOR: Isn't it? No, you're quite right. It isn't.

*The* DOCTOR *moves a door down and consults the list in his hand.*

Here he is.

JAMES *looks through the window and from his point of view we see an elderly man lying in bed, eyes and mouth open, staring blankly, clearly the victim of a stroke.*

JAMES *pushes the door and goes in.*

## 48. Interior. Hospital. Private room. Day.

JAMES *sits down and stares at his father blankly.*

*Cut to his face, then from his* FATHER's *face back to* JAMES's *face, staring at his* FATHER, *appalled.*

*Cut to a shot of the two of them and hold on to this, suggesting time passing.*

*Cut to* JAMES's *face. Suddenly remembering, he looks down at his watch, rises quickly, and goes out. He glances in through the window at his* FATHER, *then hurries along the corridor.*

## 49. Interior. Hospital. Doctor's Office. Day.

JAMES *enters. The doctor sits behind a desk.*

DOCTOR: Are you all right?

JAMES: Well, it's all been – been something of a shock. Last thing I expected.

DOCTOR: Yes, well that's the thing with strokes. They strike without – without, um – (*gestures. Pause.*) We'll let you know when there's any, um, dramatic change. It shouldn't be too long.

JAMES (*nods*): Well I'd better be getting back.

*He makes for the door, and turns.*

Oh by the way, perhaps you could help me. I had an appointment with my own doctor — today, as a matter of fact to get a prescription but of course I've — um — I've missed it.

DOCTOR: What was the prescription for?

JAMES: Sleeping pills. I've had some rather bad nights recently and — and now of course, with this.

DOCTOR: Ah. Well I really think the best thing is for you to see your own doctor, you know, first thing tomorrow. You see, I make it a principle never to prescribe except for my own patients.

JAMES: But what about tonight — my getting to sleep?

DOCTOR: Well why don't you try a cup of camomile tea and a good book. It always works for me.

JAMES *is about to say something, but hurries out.*

**50. Interior. Oxford psychological laboratory. Day.**

*Animal noises as before and come in on BORIS in a lab coat. He holds down a frenzied creature with one hand and with the other injects it with a syringe. We cannot see the creature.*

BORIS (*injecting*): We've driven the poor brute completely mad. It's got a vicious bite . . . but we'll soon have you out of it, won't we. What do you want them for?

*Cut to JAMES.*

JAMES: Well, to get some sleep, obviously.

BORIS: But you never have any trouble with sleep. You don't even have dreams. You boast about it.

JAMES: Yes, well I'm having trouble now.

*The creature is rigid but still not seen. BORIS picks it up and takes it over to the fridge. He puts the animal into the fridge and closes the door.*

Of course you realize, James, that what you're asking is quite illegal.

**51. Interior. College. Stairs. Day.**

JAMES *runs up the stairs to his rooms. He glances at his watch. It is 7.15 p.m. He opens the door.*

**52. Interior. James's bathroom. Day**

JAMES *hurries into the bathroom, grabs a glass from the drinks table outside, hesitates, grabs another, then goes back into the bathroom. He takes two pills out of his pocket and looks up.*

*He sees his face in the cabinet mirror, stares at it in surprise, then opens the cabinet door to avoid his reflection. He opens one of the capsules and shakes the contents into one of the glasses.*

DEREK (*over*): Oh, you're in there.

*As JAMES freezes.*

I knocked but you weren't there. So I thought I'd have a quick pee.

JAMES: I won't be a minute. Right out. Just going to have a gargle. Raw throat.

DEREK *enters the bathroom.*

JAMES *attempts to block the glasses from DEREK's view. He opens the cabinet door and takes out a bottle.*

DEREK (*undoing trousers*): What sort of gargle do you use?

JAMES: This one.

*He pours the bottle into a glass from the cabinet. DEREK begins to pee. We hear the sound of JAMES gargling and DEREK peeing.*

DEREK *finishes peeing and comes over to the sink.*

DEREK: Excuse me.

JAMES *continues desperately to gargle as* DEREK *shoves his fingers under the tap.*

Old nursery habit. Can't break it. Do you mind if I use your telephone?

JAMES *gargles and shakes his head.* DEREK *withdraws.* JAMES *speeds up the gargling, picks up the other capsule, hand shaking, and empties it into the other glass. He takes both glasses into the sitting room, holding them down.*

**53. Interior. James's sitting room. Day.**

DEREK *speaks urgently in a low, inaudible voice into the telephone, his back half-turned towards* JAMES. JAMES *saunters past him, puts the two glasses behind other glasses and moves away as* DEREK *hangs up.*

DEREK, *though obviously tense, tries for a smile.*

JAMES (*smiling back*): Everything all right?

DEREK: Yes, fine.

JAMES: Right, I'll pour us a drink, what would you like?

DEREK: A scotch if you've got one.

JAMES: Yes, I have. A malt?

DEREK: Perfect.

JAMES *picks up one of the two glasses and pours in some malt. Granules of powder are visible. He whirls the whisky around frantically. The whisky becomes clouded. He pours in more whisky and desperately continues to whisk the drink.*

JAMES: And how is — Penny?

DEREK (*over*): Oh, seems a bit on edge. Had another bad night. Nightmares — that sort of thing.

*Cut to the whisky, still cloudy, a few specks of powder still visible.* JAMES *continues to whisk.*

JAMES: I'm sorry to hear it.

DEREK: Yes. Consequently I had a pretty bad night myself. Didn't get much sleep either.

JAMES: Oh.

*He gives the whisky to* DEREK.

Well, let's hope this evening's a success, eh?

DEREK *lifts his glass and looks down into it. He frowns.*

(*Quickly.*) I'll be very interested to hear your views on that, by the way. It's a Glenmuldoon, the distillers only do a thousand bottles, and three hundred come to this college, one of my little coups on the wine committee.

DEREK (*sips*): Rather odd.

JAMES: Isn't it? And have you thought out your strategy?

DEREK: Mmmm?

JAMES: With my uncle.

**54. Interior. Senior Common Room. Night.**

*Various dons stand around talking, holding glasses of port, brandy etc. Among them, see* POTTS *and* DEREK *from* JAMES's *point of view.* POTTS *tells off points on the fingers of one hand.* DEREK *stares at* POTTS's *fingers. Suddenly, unable to control himself, his mouth gapes in an enormous yawn.* DEREK *forces his mouth shut, makes a Herculean effort to concentrate, then suddenly yawns again and shakes his head.*

POTTS *says something polite, turns and leaves* DEREK. *See* DEREK *shake his head muzzily and watch, as* POTTS *goes over to* JAMES.

POTTS: Amazing. Even more ill-mannered in the flesh than in his prose.

JAMES: Yes, terribly sorry, Potts. And thanks.

POTTS *squeezes his arm.*

POTTS: By the way, any news from me baby brother-in-law.

JAMES: Mmmm?

POTTS: Your father. How is he, do you know?

JAMES: Oh, still clinging on as far as I know.

POTTS (*puzzled*): Clinging on?

JAMES (*gives a little laugh*): Yes, well — um — you know what he's like.

*During this* POTTS *looks with distaste towards* DEREK *who stumbles dozily towards them.*

POTTS: Well I've been meaning to give him a ring . . .

*He squeezes* JAMES's *arm as* DEREK, *yawning is almost upon them.*

### 55. Interior. James's sitting room. Night.

*The camera comes in on* DEREK *in an armchair, yawning. It then includes* JAMES *in the shot. He stands by the drinks table.*

DEREK: I don't know what the hell's the matter with me, must be last night catching up.

JAMES: Oh, don't worry. He thinks you're charming. He told me so when he left. What'll you have? There's brandy, port, malt of course —

DEREK: Nothing for me, thanks. I already feel as if I'm in the middle of a hangover.

JAMES: Ah. Then I've got just the thing.

*With his back to* DEREK, *he pours a large amount of vodka into a glass.*

DEREK (*over*): But I'm sure he said something about going to Cambridge next week.

JAMES *picks up a bottle of Fernibranca.*

JAMES: Really?

DEREK: But I thought the point of all this was his going to the States —

JAMES, *about to pour in Fernibranca, falters slightly.*

JAMES: Yes, he is. But he's terrified of flying. So he tells everybody he's going somewhere he doesn't have to fly to. But he usually ends up on the 'plane, here you are.

DEREK (*taking it automatically*): What i it?

JAMES: It's called a Witch's Nipple in Argentina, where I'm told they drink it all the time. Became particularly popular after the Falklands' war, wher they had a lot of hangovers to deal with. Filthy taste, but it works. You have to take it down in one gulp virtually —

DEREK: Right. Thanks. I certainly need something to clear my head because I've got a hell of a night ahead of me.

JAMES: What?

DEREK: That guest room. I've got a use for it after all.

JAMES: Oh, you're going to stay the night then, terrific.

DEREK: No, I'm not. I'm going to London. Look, I'll have to trust you. There's someone that's turning awkward. Bloody awkward as a matter of fact, leaving messages at College, 'phoning me at home, making threats. Last night, for instance — just as you suspected. Anyway, if I don't go down there tonight she'll be up here doing her worst first thing tomorrow. So you're going to have to lie for me. I told Penny I'm spending the night here — she wants me to anyway. Needless to say if she ever found out — even got the slightest whiff —

JAMES: I wouldn't dream of saying a word.

DEREK: Right. Thanks. If she 'phones at all, and knowing her she probably will

JAMES: I'll say you're safely tucked up in the guest room, there's no 'phone there.

DEREK: Right. And I'll look in on my way back in the morning. To see if she's left any message I should know about.

JAMES: And if I'm out I'll leave it there. On the desk.

DEREK: Right. Well, I'd better get moving. Thank God my head's beginning to clear. I hope this stuff finishes the job.

*He throws his head back and swallows the drink. JAMES, realising too late, makes a small move to check him.*

(*Shudders.*) Anything that tastes this vile can only be good for you.

*He puts the glass down.*

Thanks for your help. I appreciate it.

*He leaves.*

JAMES *stands for a moment.*

*We see DEREK emerge into the court. He walks quickly. Takes a sudden lurching step to one side, straightens himself and goes on resolutely.*

JAMES *gets up and goes over to the telephone. He dials.*

JAMES: Hello, it's um Porker. He's just gone – to bed, of course. I filled him full of booze and – so forth, so I'm sure he'll go out like a light. We're safe until the morning. (*Little pause.*) Yes, I'm on my way right now. Oh, we'll need shovels, and – and a torch and – anything else you can think of. Something to wrap him in.

**56. Exterior/Interior. Car. Cottage drive. Night.**

JAMES *drives carefully down the drive. The front door is open and PENNY stands at it. JAMES gets out of the car and walks to the front door.*

PENNY *wears a raincoat and waterproof hat. There are two spades by the door and some sheets.*

JAMES: Well – we'd better get to it. You – you don't have to come.

PENNY: Oh yes I do. I've got to see him gone. See for myself.

JAMES: All right. Well then. We sally forth, eh?

*He picks up the two shovels.*

Why are you wearing all that?

PENNY: It might rain.

JAMES: What are those?

PENNY (*has picked up sheets*): Sheets. For wrapping him in. You said –

JAMES: But won't they be identifiable? If he's found –

PENNY: But they're only sheets. Ordinary sheets. The sort you can get –

JAMES: What's that?

*He points to embroidery on the corner.*

PENNY: What – oh, our initials. It must be the pair Derek's mother gave us. I'll get some others.

JAMES: No sheets.

PENNY: But I haven't got anything else.

JAMES: Nothing is better than sheets.

PENNY: It's only that you said –

JAMES: Let's go.

**57. Exterior. The cottage lawn. Night.**

JAMES *and* PENNY *walk across the lawn in the moonlight.*

PENNY: Where shall we put him?

JAMES: If we move him somewhere the other side of the ditch – there's some ground there, isn't there?

PENNY: Oh no. No no. I can't have him on our property.

JAMES: But Patch –

PENNY: He shouldn't have been there in the first place. That's why the whole thing started. If he's going to be lying under our ground, rotting away — poisoning me —

JAMES: But we can't move him far. I'm not going to move him far. It's too dangerous.

PENNY: In that case, why bother to do it at all? If you can't help me *properly* — (*She stops.*)

JAMES *stares at her.*

## 58.  Exterior. The woods. Undergrowth. Night.

*Shot of* PILKINGTON's *body being dragged through the undergrowth.*

*Cut to* JAMES's *face, straining.*

JAMES: Is this far enough?

PENNY (*shines torch ahead*): Just a bit more. Another few yards, or so.

## 59.  Exterior. The woods. Small clearing. Night.

PENNY *shines the torch around.*

PENNY: Here. A very nice spot.

JAMES, *sweating, nods.*

I probably wouldn't be able to find it even, in daytime.

JAMES *nods.*

*Cut to* JAMES *digging.*

PENNY *shines the torch on him. She sits quite comfortably under a tree. It is raining.*

Yes, it said on the radio it was going to. I expect it's making the ground softer. Is it?

JAMES *continues to dig. He is soaked, dirty.*

*Cut to later. A shot of the deep grave.*

*Cut to* PILKINGTON, *then to* JAMES. *He pulls* PILKINGTON *to the lip of*

the grave, makes a supreme effort, and rolls him in.

JAMES *looks down and from his point of view we see for the first time that* PILKINGTON's *body is covered in cuts.*

JAMES *frowns, as though he realises something, then puts the thought away. He bends and throws the scissors down.*

*Cut to* JAMES *who sits beside* PENNY *under a tree, exhausted.*

It's stopped raining, at least.

JAMES: Yes.

PENNY: They said it would only be a shower. (*After a moment.*) Hadn't we better get on with the last bit. Then we're done.

*Cut to* PILKINGTON's *body, the scissors on his face. A spadeful of earth covers it.*

*Cut to* JAMES. *He packs down the grave then stands heaving, resting on his shovel.*

(*Flashes light over it.*) It looks very fresh.

JAMES: It is fresh.

PENNY: Well, we'd better put something over it.

JAMES *is pulling up briars, then digging them up and sticking them on the grave, illuminated by* PENNY's *torch.*

What do you think?

JAMES, *near collapse, leans on his shovel.*

JAMES: Fine. Fine. Just fine.

PENNY: Yes.

JAMES *throws her a glance of relief.*

There you are, Horace. At rest at last. No more lying about in a ditch. Thou thy worldly task hast done, home art gone, and taken thy wages.

*She looks at* JAMES.

JAMES: It's ta'en. Not taken. Ta'en thy wages. Not taken thy —

*He gestures, exhaustedly.*

### 60. Exterior. The cottage lawn. Dawn.

JAMES *and* PENNY *walk across the lawn.* JAMES *is dragging the two shovels,* PENNY *is carrying the torch.*

### 61. Exterior. The Cottage. Dawn.

PENNY *puts the spades against the cottage wall and opens the front door.*

JAMES *makes as if to follow.*

PENNY (*turning, stops him*): No, just a minute. (*Looks at him.*) You're a terrible mess. You should have worn something over. You'd better get undressed here, otherwise you'll be tramping mud all over the house. I'll go and run you a bath — unless you'd rather have a bath at your own place?

JAMES: No.

PENNY *takes off her raincoat, hat, wellingtons, etc. and goes up stairs as* JAMES *begins to undress.*

### 62. Interior. The Cottage. Stairs. Dawn.

JAMES, *in his underwear, climbs the stairs, seen from below. He is wet to the skin.*

### 63. Interior. The Cottage. Bathroom. Dawn.

JAMES *enters.* PENNY *is there, putting out a towel. The bath is run. Foamy.*

PENNY: There's your towel. And I've put in lots of bath bubbles. Why are you still in your knickers? Give them to me.

JAMES *hesitates, then steps out of his underpants and hands them to* PENNY.

Right, in you get. I'll find you some clothes.

*Cut to* JAMES, *almost asleep in the bath. The water is filthy.*

PENNY *appears at the door. She is seen blearily, from* JAMES's *point of view.*

(*Looks at bath.*) Run it out, shower it down, run yourself another one. Here. (*Hands him a mug.*) You should have showered first. It's a rum toddy. (*Withdraws, reappears.*) Clothes are in the bedroom.

### 64. Interior. The Cottage. Stairs to bedroom. Day.

JAMES, *a towel around his waist, goes up the stairs, seen from below. He enters the bedroom.*

### 65. Interior. The Cottage. Bedroom. Day.

PENNY *sits on the bed, cross-legged. She sews, a work-basket beside her.*

JAMES *stands at the door gazing at her.*

JAMES: What — what are you doing?

PENNY: Sewing a button on Derek's shirt.

JAMES: Oh.

PENNY *looks up at him and smiles.*

PENNY: It's for you. I can't give you one of his good ones, he always knows exactly about his clothes, but there are some he's thrown out for Help the Aged, but I took all the buttons off them, now I'm having to put some back on. Serves me right for being so mean —

*She looks up at him and grins.*

— you can put on the rest of them — there.

PENNY *indicates a pile of clothes on the bed with* JAMES's *wallet, keys, etc. beside them.*

I've put your belt through the trousers, they're a bit ragged but they'll get you home – and there are your dirty ones –

*She indicates a plastic dustbin liner.*

JAMES *stands.*

Well, go on, get dressed, I won't be a minute. I've given you his flip flops –

*As* JAMES *begins to get dressed.*

– he won't miss those, I think they're Turkish – there we are! (*Cutting thread.*) How are you doing? (*Looks at him.*)

*Cut to a few minutes later.*

JAMES *is togged out in* DEREK's *clothes. He puts the wallet, keys etc. in the pockets. The clothes are too big for him. He looks preposterous. The shirt has only one button.*

That's all right. Well, they'll do to get you back.

JAMES: Can I really walk across New Court like this?

PENNY: Of course you can. You look perfectly –

*She shrieks with laughter.*

Sorry. Sorry. It's just that I can scarcely believe – I still really haven't taken in – my head feels so – I mean, he's actually gone. For good. Gone. Gone. Gone. Gone. Gone. We did it, didn't we?

*She looks at him with glowing eyes.*

JAMES (*grins*): Yes, we did. Just like the old – old days. You lead. I follow. But not to any corpses next time, please Patch.

PENNY: Porker, I think you're wonderful.

JAMES: Do you?

PENNY: Yes, I do. Quite wonderful. And adorable with it.

*She kisses him on the cheek.*

JAMES *puts his arms around her. He strokes her hair.*

JAMES: Oh, my Patch! My Patch! Do you know – do you know what you mean to me? Have always meant to me? I think – ever since that summer – all these years I've been locked in some little cell, hunched in some little cell – I must have been waiting for you to come back, and let me out – I love you. (*Kisses her.*) Love you.

PENNY: What are you doing?

JAMES (*kisses her again*): I'm not going to let you go again – ever. You're mine. (*Kisses her again.*)

PENNY (*steps away*): You can't. (*Little laugh.*) You can't.

JAMES: Why not?

PENNY: Well, for one thing, you're homosexual.

JAMES: What! (*Laughs.*) Don't be ridiculous.

PENNY: But you are. Derek told me. He said you were Boris's boyfriend, sort of, as far as he could make out. And anyway, he said you admitted it yourself, he said you were quite open about it. He said – (*looks at him*)

JAMES: How could you of all people – you of all people. I only let Derek believe it for – for your sake.

PENNY: For my sake!

JAMES: So he wouldn't mind my – our – seeing each other. But you can't – you can't ever have thought – no. You didn't. Not in your heart, you didn't. (*Steps forward.*)

PENNY: But I haven't thought about you in my heart. I never think about anyone in my heart except Derek. I thought you understood that, Piglet.

JAMES: Porker. It's Porker. There was someone called Piglet wasn't there? Someone else. It's not just the names you keep confusing.

PENNY: Well, there might have been – I

think there was — another boy the summer before or after. He wasn't anything as nice as you, though. (*Smiles.*) I remember you far better. But now I really think you'd better go, you know. It's getting late — early, I mean. We've both got to get some rest and Derek might come back early and —

JAMES: No, I'm not going. I can't. You don't love him. You can't. I've seen the way he talks to you, the way he looks at you — or doesn't look at you. His indifference, his rudeness. And you say yourself you're frightened of him. What has he done to deserve you?

PENNY: Oh, Porker, you don't know anything about it. (*Laughs.*) He loves me. We have a happy, happy marriage.

JAMES: A happy marriage? (*Laughs.*) Oh Patch, you know what sort of man he is.

PENNY: Yes I do. And I don't want you to say another — not another —

JAMES: Do you know where he is now? He's not asleep in my College, he's gone down to London to see one of his barmaids, that girl who called last night, Liz . . . she's been making trouble. He sat in my room telling me all about her because he wanted me to lie to you.

PENNY (*shaking her head*): It's not true, it's not true. (*Turns away.*)

JAMES: Yes it is. Why, even Boris knows all about him. In London he was known as the ram. I know it isn't in the rules to tell on husbands, but I'm not playing by the rules. I'd do anything for you, Patch. Anything but let you go. I wasn't just sent to you to help you. You were sent to me because I need you. So I can start my life at last. I have always needed you. (*Moves towards her.*)

PENNY *turns around. On her face, a grimace of loathing.*

JAMES *stands in shock.*

PENNY: You're worse than Pilkington, worse, you should have buried yourself with him, buried yourself, he just put his hands on me, but you — lie and lie and lie about everything, everything —

*She runs at him and attacks him with her fingers, scratching and punching.*

hate you, hate you, hate you —

JAMES *tries desperately to get away.*

PENNY *continues to assault him.*

JAMES, *back against the bed, falls on to it.* PENNY *scrambles after him on her hands and knees and as she does so, sees the scissors from her work-basket knocked over by* JAMES. *She grabs them.*

JAMES: No — no — no — no —

*As* PENNY *pursues him, stabbing viciously but only making contact with his clothes, not his body.*

### 66. Interior. The Cottage. Stairs and Hall. Day.

JAMES, *impeded by flip-flops and baggy trousers, tumbles downstairs, pursued by* PENNY. *He scrambles to his feet, through the door.*

### 67. Exterior. The cottage drive. Day.

JAMES *scrambles to his car and manages to get in. He shuts the door and locks it, just before* PENNY *reaches him.*

*She runs around the car to the other door.*

JAMES *leans across and locks it in the nick of time, then, as she runs around and around the car, snarling in at him, seemingly everywhere, he fumbles his keys out of his pocket and gets the car started.*

*From his point of view, as the car leaps down the drive, see* PENNY *running after it, jabbing the scissors up and down.*

*She throws back her head and gives a hideous scream.*

### 68. Interior. Boris's rooms. College. Day.

*Come in first on* BORIS *in his pyjamas, at his door. He is just aroused from sleep.*

*Cut to* JAMES *staring at him.*

### 69. Interior. Oxford psychology lab. Day.

BORIS *has dressed as if hastily.*

JAMES: And another thing. When I was burying Pilkington — I suddenly noticed there were gashes all over him — not just in his neck. So she slaughtered him just as she tried to slaughter me.

BORIS: Yes, well she's quite evidently gone mad. Far madder than you've gone, even.

JAMES: Look, what precisely are we going to do?

BORIS: First obviously calm her down. Then phone a shrink of my acquaintance, give him a highly edited version of the facts and get her hospitalised immediately. Then we'll have to work out how to save you from jail and Penny from a lifetime in an institute for the criminally insane. Also how much we tell Derek. If he's survived the night, that is. (*Grins at* JAMES.)

BORIS *has been packing his briefcase. He checks a syringe professionally.*

JAMES: What's that?

BORIS: A sedative.

BORIS *packs a bottle and pad.*

JAMES: What's that?

BORIS: Chloroform.

JAMES: But if you've got a sedative —

BORIS: Yes, but I may have to subdue her first. Especially if she comes at me with her scissors —

*He turns off the lights.*

### 70. Exterior. The cottage drive. Day.

*A car goes slowly down the drive. It is past dawn. Birds are twittering and so forth.*

### 71. Interior/Exterior. Car. The cottage drive. Day.

BORIS *parks the car.*

*They look towards the house.*

*See the house from their point of view. The front door is closed.*

JAMES: You will be careful, won't you?

BORIS: My dear James, I have to deal with frenzied monkeys all the time.

JAMES: No, I meant — be careful with her.

BORIS *looks at* JAMES *and laughs slightly.*

BORIS: Good God, James!

JAMES: I wish you weren't enjoying it all so much.

*He looks at* BORIS.

BORIS *looks towards the house.*

*We see it from their point of view. The door is now slightly ajar.*

BORIS: Is the door open?

JAMES: Yes.

BORIS: Was it a minute ago?

JAMES: I don't know. I think so, yes.

BORIS: Good. Then I might take her unawares.

*He makes a move to get out of the car.* JAMES *does also.*

No, you stay here.

JAMES: I'm coming with you.

BORIS: You're not James. It's you she wants to kill, don't forget. I'll call you when I'm ready.

*He gets out and walks briskly to the door. pushes it open carefully, and slides smoothly into the house.*

*Pause.*

*See the house from* JAMES's *point of view. The front door opens and* BORIS *reappears. The door slams behind him.*

BORIS *walks back to the car, grinning, and leans against* JAMES's *window which* JAMES *lowers.*

BORIS: She was waiting for me behind the door. Must have been the car. Thought I was you – (*Grins.*) – help me, please, eh? Help me.

*He falls to the ground.*

JAMES *opens the door with difficulty.* BORIS, *hideously gashed, has a pair of scissors sticking from his neck. He is dying.*

JAMES *gets out of the car and walks slowly towards the house. He stands at the door, hesitates, then tries the knob. The door opens.*

### 72. Interior. Cottage hall and stairs. Day.

JAMES *goes in cautiously, looking behind the door. No-one there.* BORIS's *case is on the floor.*

JAMES *closes his eyes in terror as a faint sound is heard above. He looks up the stairs, hesitates, then goes up quietly.*

*He approaches the bedroom door. It is half open. He pushes it open more fully.* PENNY *is sitting on the edge of the bed, hands folded in her lap.*

*She stares at* JAMES *for a moment.*

### 73. Interior. Cottage bedroom. Day.

JAMES: Hello, Patch.

PENNY: Oh, hello Piglet. I knew you were all right, really. I knew I could never hurt you, could I?

JAMES: No Patch, you couldn't.

PENNY: I was just going to go downstairs to make sure. And then here you are. So I don't have to now, do I?

JAMES: No, Patch, you don't.

*He goes over and sits down beside her.*

PENNY: Oh, it's so good to see you, Piglet, alive and well. I'm awfully tired. I've had such a strange time recently. Shall I go to bed now?

JAMES: Yes, I think you should.

PENNY: Would you help me, please? Such a long night it's been, you see. Up to all kinds of things, haven't we?

JAMES: Yes, we have. Here. Stand up, Patch. And let's get you tucked in, shall we?

PENNY *stands up.*

JAMES *helps* PENNY *to get undressed, beginning with her shoes.*

JAMES (*undoing shoes*): Lift up, there's a good girl. Now the other one. There. And now your dress. (*Unbuttons it.*) Just slip your arms – (*Puts dress over chair.*) – keeps it neatly so it doesn't crease.

*He goes behind her, unclips her bra and puts it over a chair.*

And now just –

*He pulls down her pants.*

*She steps out of them.*

*He looks at her and we see her from his point of view.*

Where are your night things, under the pillow?

PENNY: Under the pillow, yes.

JAMES *lifts up the pillow.* DEREK's *pyjamas. He lifts up the other pillow.* PENNY's *nightdress.*

JAMES: Lift your arms then, Patch.

PENNY *does.*

Now (*Turning back covers.*) In you get.

PENNY (*crosses to bed. Stops*): Oh, but I haven't brushed my teeth. Do you think it matters?

JAMES: No, not this once, Patch, it doesn't.

PENNY: No, once won't hurt.

*She gets into bed.*

*JAMES comes and sits on the edge of the bed.*

(*After a pause.*) I don't want to go through any of that again, Piglet. Not ever. I'm too old now.

JAMES: Yes. (*Takes her hand.*) So am I.

PENNY: You won't let it happen again then?

JAMES: No.

PENNY: Do you promise?

JAMES: I promise, Patch.

PENNY: Goodnight then, Piglet.

JAMES (*gently*): It's Porker.

PENNY: Yes. Sorry. Goodnight Porker.

JAMES: Goodnight Patch.

*Cut to the two, hands enfolded.*

*Then cut to PENNY's face. She is asleep, but restless, murmuring.*

*Cut to JAMES's face, looking down on hers. JAMES releases her hand and gets up.*

### 74.   Interior. Cottage stairs. Day.

JAMES *goes down the stairs. He opens BORIS's case and takes out the chloroform and the pad.*

### 75.   Interior. Cottage bedroom. Day.

JAMES *sits down on the edge of the bed and pours some chloroform onto the pad. He puts the pad to PENNY's nose.*

*She is still sleeping restlessly. She inhales several times then goes into a deeper sleep. Her face is calm and untroubled.*

JAMES *screws the cap back on the bottle then puts the pad and bottle in his pocket.*

*See PENNY's face from his point of view. He picks up DEREK's pillow and puts it over PENNY's face, holding it firmly but gently.*

*Cut to JAMES's face looking down at PENNY, then to PENNY dead.*

JAMES *kisses her on the forehead and turns to go. As he does so, his eye catches the dustbin liner with his clothes inside. He picks it up.*

### 76.   Exterior. The Cottage. Day.

JAMES *bends to examine BORIS beside the car. He is clearly dead. JAMES walks round the other side of the car, gets in and drives off, being careful to avoid BORIS's body.*

### 77.   Exterior. Hertford College. New Court. Day.

*It is about nine in the morning. JAMES is walking across the court, carrying a bag of clothes. He cuts a bizarre figure, still in DEREK's togs.*

*He is noticed by various people as they pass him.*

*He turns into his stairway.*

### 78.   Interior. James's rooms. Day.

JAMES *enters, drops the bag on the floor and goes towards the bedroom/bathroom. As he makes to open the door there is a sound from the armchair.*

*He turns and from his point of view we see a figure heaving himself out of the armchair. It is DEREK, eyes bloodshot, unshaven. He stands looking at JAMES, swaying slightly.*

DEREK (*dully*): Just checked in to see if she phoned. Nothing on the desk.

JAMES: No.

DEREK: Then made the mistake of
 sitting down for a minute. I had a sort
 of — of black-out on the motorway.
 Felt myself going so I pulled into a
 layby. Out for hours. By the time I
 got to her place she had left. Just hope
 to God she hasn't come up here. To
 make trouble on my doorstep. Well,
 at least no messages, eh?

JAMES: No, no messages.

*He goes to the door, turns, and looks
at JAMES, clearly noticing something
odd about his appearance. He frowns.*

*He turns to go out, turns back, looks
at JAMES once more and again frowns
slightly at his appearance.*

*JAMES goes to the window and looks
down. From his point of view we see
DEREK walking doggedly across the
court.*

*Ends.*

Titles published by Methuen
in the Modern Plays series
are listed overleaf.

| | |
|---|---|
| Barrie Keeffe | *Gimme Shelter (Gem, Gotcha, Getaway)* |
| | *Barbarians (Killing Time, Abide With Me, In the City)* |
| | *A Mad World, My Masters* |
| Arthur Kopit | *Indians* |
| | *Wings* |
| Larry Kramer | *The Normal Heart* |
| John McGrath | *The Cheviot, the Stag and the Black, Black Oil* |
| David Mamet | *Glengarry Glen Ross* |
| | *American Buffalo* |
| David Mercer | *After Haggerty* |
| | *Cousin Vladimir* and *Shooting the Chandelier* |
| | *Duck Song* |
| | *The Monster of Karlovy Vary* and *Then and Now* |
| | *No Limits To Love* |
| Arthur Miller | *The American Clock* |
| | *The Archbishop's Ceiling* |
| | *Two-Way Mirror* |
| | *Danger: Memory!* |
| Percy Mtwa | |
| Mbongeni Ngema | *Woza Albert!* |
| Barney Simon | |
| Peter Nichols | *Passion Play* |
| | *Poppy* |
| Joe Orton | *Loot* |
| | *What the Butler Saw* |
| | *Funeral Games* and *The Good and Faithful Servant* |
| | *Entertaining Mr Sloane* |
| | *Up Against It* |
| Louise Page | *Golden Girls* |
| Harold Pinter | *The Birthday Party* |
| | *The Room* and *The Dumb Waiter* |
| | *The Caretaker* |
| | *A Slight Ache and other plays* |
| | *The Collection* and *The Lover* |

|                   | The Homecoming |
|-------------------|----------------|
|                   | Tea Party and other plays |
|                   | Landscape and Silence |
|                   | Old Times |
|                   | No Man's Land |
|                   | Betrayal |
|                   | The Hothouse |
|                   | Other Places (A Kind of Alaska, Victoria Station, Family Voices) |
| Luigi Pirandello  | Henry IV |
|                   | Six Characters in Search of an Author |
| Sephen Poliakoff  | Coming in to Land |
|                   | Hitting Town and City Sugar |
|                   | Breaking the Silence |
| David Rudkin      | The Saxon Shore |
|                   | The Sons of Light |
|                   | The Triumph of Death |
| Jean-Paul Sartre  | Crime Passionnel |
| Wole Soyinka      | Madmen and Specialists |
|                   | The Jero Plays |
|                   | Death and the King's Horseman |
|                   | A Play of Giants |
| C. P. Taylor      | And a Nighingale Sang . . . |
|                   | Good |
| Peter Whelan      | The Accrington Pals |
| Nigel Williams    | Line 'Em |
|                   | Class Enemy |
| Theatre Workshop  | Oh What a Lovely War! |
| Various authors   | Best Radio Plays of 1978 (Don Haworth: Episode on a Thursday Evening; Tom Mallin: Halt! Who Goes There?; Jennifer Phillips: Daughters of Men; Fay Weldon: Polaris; Jill Hyem: Remember Me; Richard Harris: Is It Something I Said?) |
|                   | Best Radio Plays of 1979 (Shirley Gee: Typhoid Mary; Carey Harrison: I Never Killed My German; Barrie Keeffe: Heaven Scent; |

John Kirkmorris: *Coxcombe;* John
Peacock: *Attard in Retirement;* Olwen
Wymark: *The Child*)

*Best Radio Plays of 1981* (Peter Barnes:
*The Jumping Mimuses of Byzantium;*
Don Haworth: *Talk of Love and War;*
Harold Pinter: *Family Voices;* David
Pownall: *Beef;* J P Rooney: *The Dead
Image;* Paul Thain: *The Biggest
Sandcastle in the World*)

*Best Radio Plays of 1982* (Rhys
Adrian: *Watching the Plays Together;*
John Arden: *The Old Man Sleeps
Alone;* Harry Barton: *Hoopoe Day;*
Donald Chapman: *Invisible Writing;*
Tom Stoppard: *The Dog It Was
That Died;* William Trevor: *Autumn
Sunshine*)

*Best Radio Plays of 1983* (Wally K Daly:
*Time Slip;* Shirley Gee: *Never in My
Lifetime;* Gerry Jones: *The Angels They
Grow Lonely;* Steve May: *No
Exceptions;* Martyn Read: *Scouting for
Boys*)

*Best Radio Plays of 1984* (Stephen
Dunstone: *Who Is Sylvia?;* Don
Haworth: *Daybreak;* Robert Ferguson:
*Transfigured Night;* Caryl Phillips:
*The Wasted Years;* Christopher Russell:
*Swimmer;* Rose Tremain: *Temporary
Shelter*)

*Best Radio Plays of 1985* (Rhys
Adrian: *Outpatient;* Barry
Collins: *King Canute;* Martin
Crimp: *The Attempted Acts;*
David Pownall: *Ploughboy
Monday;* James Saunders:
*Menocchio;* Michael Wall:
*Hiroshima: The Movie*)